OTHER BOOKS BY KAREN MAINS

Karen, Karen
Key to a Loving Heart
Making Sunday Special
Open Heart, Open Home
The Fragile Curtain
The God Hunt: A Discovery Book for Children
With My Whole Heart
You Are What You Say

CO-AUTHORED BOOKS

Child Sexual Abuse: A Hope for Healing
Living, Loving, Leading
Parenting Us: How God Does It
Tales of the Kingdom
Tales of the Resistance
The God Hunt: A Discovery Book for Men and Women

Friends AND Strangers

Divine Encounters in Lonely Places

KAREN BURTON MAINS

WORD PUBLISHING
Dallas·London·Vancouver·Melbourne

FRIENDS AND STRANGERS:
DIVINE ENCOUNTERS IN LONELY PLACES

Scripture quotations used in this book are from the following sources:
    The King James Version of the Bible (KJV).
    The Revised Standard Version of the Bible (RSV), copyrighted
        1946, 1952, © 1971, 1973 by the Division of Christian Education of
        the National Council of the Churches of Christ in the U.S.A., and
        are used by permission.
    The Living Bible (TLB), copyright 1971 by Tyndale House Publishers,
        Wheaton, IL. Used by permission.

This book is about real people; names and identifying information in some cases have been changed to protect confidentiality.

Library of Congress Cataloging-in-Publication Data:

Mains, Karen Burton.
        Friends and strangers : divine encounters in lonely places / Karen
    Burton Mains.
            p. cm.
        ISBN 0-8499-0735-7
        1. Loneliness—Religious aspects—Christianity.   2. Mains, Karen
    Burton.   I. Title.
        BV4911.M35   1990
        241'.676—dc20   90–43486
                                                                                                            CIP
Printed in the United States of America

012349 AGF 987654321

To the people of St. Mark's parish
who made a home for me
on the way to my true home.

Contents

CONTENTS

Acknowledgments

My deepest gratitude
to my editors
who make my books the best they can be.

A special thanks
to
Harold Fickett—
I could not have completed this
project well without
his expert help.

PART I

Friends and Strangers

1

Friends and Strangers

The secluded road down which I take my morning walks is narrow, overhung with oak trees and pushed close by the embrace of roadside shrubs. My route takes me past the mushroom farm, past the broad lawns and horse paddocks of my more wealthy neighbors, then along the playing fields of a private high school. The school's white chapel, which rises on the far side of the playing fields, stands apart from the other buildings on campus. It seems to face the others from a lonely but morally superior position. As I go on in my walk, I cross a stream and then follow an abandoned road, which winds back toward home again.

The features of the land here, its marshes and river banks, its stands of trees and grassy fields, are remnants of an open countryside into which my family moved some thirteen years ago. Developers are felling the woods, carving up the fields, draining the marshes. It has been years since I have seen a snowy egret. Soon we will be house to house, backyard to backyard. The solace of open country will be lost forevermore. The people who move here from now on will never know what has been displaced. I remember I once saw a fawn crossing the asphalt lane: he paused and then, with a few quiet steps, he blended back into the forest's oblivion.

I push the pace of my walking on the way out, but coming back I stroll. I do not want a companion. This is one of the few times I can guarantee myself uninterrupted moments to think. I attempt great thoughts while sauntering. I memorize Emily Dickinson's poetry typed on three-by-five cards. "A light exists in spring / Not present on the Year / At any other period. . . ." Often I outline radio broadcasts that I will be taping for the ministry, "Chapel of the Air," which I share with my husband, David. I try to pray, but the world, lush in its seclusion, distracts me. I pass *Swanoaks*, my brother-in-law's acreage, and think, with some regret, of my family, how busy we all are, how I would like to stop in for coffee but don't want to intrude.

One sunny day, on the homeward leg of my walk, an old man, a gentleman farmer, rode a tractor down the road, heading toward me. He was hauling a load of compost and turned into the driveway I was approaching. Wearing a straw hat, suspendered dungarees, and a chambray work shirt, he waved and called out, "How-dee!" His smile was as bright as the day.

I answered and continued on, but was surprised by a sharp catch of pain beneath my breastbone and the surge of tears. I kept wiping my cheeks all the way home, another mile and a half. *Karen Mains*, I thought, *if you cry when an old man smiles at you, then you'd better pay attention to what's going on within.*

This incident remains with me as a kind of fable, *Old Man and the Middle-Aged Woman*, which shadows all my other tales. That brief encounter began a seven-year journey into self-recognition. Among many other things, I discovered I was a lonely woman. Lonely. That was such a hard word for me even to say at the beginning of my journey. But I have owned it. It names my pain. I am ready to speak it in the depths of my heart: I have been a lonely woman. The moral of my story: *Pay attention when strangers smile on you.*

I discovered that loneliness has nothing to do with whether you are surrounded by people. Loneliness in the middle of a crowd is so common that the title of the famous book, *The Lonely Crowd,* now seems to me a fitting description of most social circles. Loneliness is a matter of not being able to make significant human connections, something beyond running into each other at social occasions or being grouped together at work; something beyond the exchange of pleasantries and witticisms. Loneliness is helped most by kindred spirits, friends whose souls are present to one another in a way that goes beyond words.

The discovering of like-souled folk can take time. And this lack is what I often blamed for my condition. But in addition, I found out that sometimes we cannot discover soul mates because we cannot be soul mates. We cannot have intimacy with others because of a lack of intimacy within ourselves, among our trinity of body, mind, and spirit. Others neglect us because we have habitually neglected ourselves. When an old man smiled on me, I had to reckon with the strange fact that I had few friends to whom I was willing to reveal myself and the even stranger fact that I did not know what I would tell them if I were willing.

One journal entry (one of many) tells the story: "April, 1985. Lord, I don't think there are enough people in my life who are there for me. Please bring me healing friends. In the meanwhile, ease this pain, this feeling of aloneness. Give me human relationships of your choosing that are appropriate for me."

Discovering the source of loneliness is not a simple enterprise. It is rather like the ball of yarn the kitten has playfully mangled. You can scarcely find the loose end to begin unraveling. All is tangled, knotted, criss-crossed, double-tied. It took seven years in all to unravel massed snags due to my self-neglect, busyness, and accumulated pains and griefs.

I began to sense that the Karen who functioned so well in public was estranged in some way from my most private self. There was an awkward misstepping, like walking in two different shoes, one a sandal, one a high-heeled pump. The more visible my public image became (speaking to hundreds! writing for thousands! broadcasting to millions!) the more imminent my collapse due to this off-balanced stride. The struggle for proficiency—my own amazement at my success at achieving a standard of professionalism—the growing disciplines of work and learning and spirituality hid from me the fact that the public self was outdistancing the private self. Racing forward, I abandoned something, but I could hear that part of myself crying out at night, and I could sense it in vague daytime dissatisfactions. Finally the pain came to the surface.

I suppose that those of us who are lonely have chosen loneliness or at least we have made choices that have rendered us lonely. Looking back, I can see that in several crucial instances I chose self-sufficiency. I chose to be private about my own needs. When different people upon whom I depended disappointed me, I remained quiet and took care of my own problems. That became an almost unconscious pattern, which led to isolation. I forgave, I was loving; but I protected myself. I began to develop defenses which were related solely to my adult journey. No early childhood trauma here, no adolescent regression; just the fact that growing up, becoming an adult, is hard to do, and I did some of it the wrong way.

I called out to the Lord for friends, but He needed to teach me about the inappropriateness of my self-sufficiency, about my growing personal isolation, about the disparity between my proficient professional self and my lagging inner-being. So He outwitted my defenses. He continued to tutor me about my problems in the same way He captured my attention: He used strangers; those who bumped into me in unusual byways and in odd places. Their messages penetrated my heart before my defenses intercepted them.

The lonely places of my life are wildernesses into which strangers have borne bread and water. Gerard Manley Hopkins captures this mystery poetically: ". . . for Christ plays in ten thousand places / Lovely in limbs, and lovely in eyes not His / To the Father through the features of men's faces." Nowadays few glance my way without my considering whose face might be present in theirs.

Because of the brokenness of the world, we are all, to one degree or another, strangers to ourselves. Much of our inability to recognize Christ in our daily lives is due to this interior estrangement. Christ often assumes the guise of a stranger, therefore, to minister to us.

This three-sided theology of the stranger winds in and out of the stories of Scripture. In Genesis, chapter eighteen, strangers appear to Abraham and Sarah in Hebron with a divine message that appears incredible: they are, indeed, this old twosome, to impregnate and be impregnated with a promised heir. The New Testament reports a companion history. Disciples on the road to Emmaus are encountered by a stranger, the unrecognized risen Christ. Parker Palmer in his remarkable book, *The Company of Strangers*, draws parallels between these two accounts:

> In both of these stories the stranger is a bearer of truth which might not otherwise have been received. Both stories tell us that our everyday perceptions and assumptions must be shaken by the intrusion of strangeness if we are to hear God's word. . . . This function of the stranger in our lives is grounded in a simple fact: truth is a very large matter, and requires various angles of vision to be seen in the round. . . . God persistently challenges conventional truth and regularly upsets the world's way of looking at things. It is no accident that this God is so often represented by the stranger, for the truth that God speaks in our lives is very strange, indeed.

Many of us are wary of strangers. We still hear our mothers' voices, "Never talk to strangers." Strangers represent danger, potential harm. In our violent society, it is right to exercise caution. But in many circumstances, we are wary of the stranger because of the danger he represents to our own tightly held prejudices. The stranger may disrupt our self-deceptions. We know this intuitively and keep our distance. This is dangerous stuff indeed; it is shattering to be shaken by divine encounters ". . . lovely in limbs, and lovely in eyes not His. . . ."

If we are to be connected to one another in significant ways, we must pursue three courses of action simultaneously—for each course of action may prove unreal without the others. We must seek to know God; we must seek to know ourselves; and we must seek to know both God and ourselves in the company of others. My encounters with strangers have shattered my individualistic notion that I could find my own way into God alone. My spiritual journey cannot be a solo crossing. Unaided, I am frighteningly unable to know myself. Any insistence on self-sufficiency estranges me from the very Christ I seek to find.

When I was younger, young men caught my eye, signaling their admiration. Now that I am middle-aged, it is old men who smile on me. Perhaps I remind them of lost sweethearts, or of daughters, or of their wives long ago. Babies smile at me, also. Prone in their strollers or kicking their heels in shopping carts while their mothers hunt breads and cans of vegetables, they sneak looks at me, sideways glances that end in rakish grins. Women my age smile also; they nod at me, sometimes on the street or while we wait for planes. With them, I sometimes think, I share a conspiritorial knowledge. "We have kept ourselves well," their looks seem to say. "Hold your head proudly. Walk tall."

I do not take any of these encounters lightly, not any more. Who knows what gift some stranger will bring me in my lonely places? "I was a stranger," said Christ, "and you welcomed me." When I reckon with a stranger, I am reckoning with my Lord. When another treats me, a stranger, with courtesy, he reveres the image of God in which I was created. Ephesians 2 explains cryptically, "At one time . . . you were . . . separated . . . alienated . . . strangers . . . you who once were far off have been brought near in the blood of

8

Christ. For he is our peace, who has made us both one . . . that he might create in himself one new man in place of the two . . ." (vv. 11–15, RSV).

I am well aware now that the greatest secret about strangers is that any one of them may become a friend, one who will not forget me, nor abandon me when I am troubled, nor lie to me when I need the truth. All of my best friends were at one time strangers. In addition, I am a stranger; my strangeness can bring unaccountable truth to others. Who knows but what I may become their friend?

"O thou hope of Israel," asks Jeremiah, "Why should thou be like a stranger in the land, like a wayfarer who turns aside to tarry for a night?" Delusion, neglect, our own sin blind us to the One who is always in our midst. In the long run, how we receive the stranger is a test of our understanding of Christ's existential visitations, His here in this now.

The three-sided nature of identity — the person as she relates to herself, to God, and to community — is often thrust upon us by the unexpected encounter. In the following pages I will be recounting my meetings with strangers that over a seven-year period changed me in ways that helped cure my loneliness; that enabled me to choose community over individualism; that taught me to minister in new and more authentic ways; and that opened up within me God-given aspects of my personality which I had neglected and suppressed. A central, hidden self within was crying for attention and finally used pain to make me listen. Each chapter is a story about a stranger, but the themes that are woven through them are about an increasing self-recognition.

Each incident, each meeting, has had a cumulative effect on me. I have finally realized the stranger I am to myself can only find its real place in the arms of another Stranger, Jesus Christ. He is the one who outwits my self-deception by coming to me in the guise of many strangers — strangers who, once I recognize the presence of Christ within them, become my friends.

PART II

Alone with Strangers

2

The Loneliest Man
I Ever Met

The loneliest man I ever met calls me on the phone every couple of weeks, usually on Sunday evenings. The first time he called, I could scarcely understand him; he stuttered, triple-tonguing every explosive consonant. At first, my understanding was hampered by his speech disability; then I could hardly believe what I finally understood him to be saying. My caller complained that no church woman's sewing circle would allow him membership. "He didn't b-b-belong in the m-m-men's group. W-w-women were mo-mo-more cr-cr-creative; they d-d-did h-h-handiwork. Th-th-they g-g-got tasks d-d-d-one. If only th-th-they were fr-fr-friendlier."

In the whole city of Chicago, it seemed, there was not a single church women's club with room for James O'Brady. No Women's Missionary Society, no Women's Baptist Union, no United Methodist Women's group, no one, would have him. James either ran into stereotypical sexist thinking, or, as I learned later, his behavior was so offensive that he was eventually excluded from all the circles to which he gained a trial admission.

Obviously, as I came to learn, James thought differently from much of the world, male or female. For one thing, I have never met another man whose sole measurement of social success was acceptance within a women's sewing circle. James languished, lost in the lonely desert of his own unfulfilled expectations. A women's church society represented his Eden; and after masterminding many intriguing campaigns in order to nudge his way through the narrow entrances, he was invariably expelled on grounds of improper behavior. And every Sunday evening when he called, stammering his way through a litany of grievances, my own frustration mounted over his chronicle of rebuffs.

James O'Brady had a cause of sorts—to make the insensitive realize the plight of the lonely. He understood loneliness, for he was trapped in a double-duty isolation, walled about with loneliness and impervious to instructions in courtesy. Anticipating holiday angst, he began angling for invitations weeks before Thanksgiving and Christmas. He would not settle for an institution-alized meal served up at the Salvation Army or some downtown mission. He wanted a surrogate family, gathered around what he hoped would be a candlelit "European-style" dinner table which should groan with traditional dishes presented on heirloom silver and china. He fantasized hungrily about this dream-world, which receded ever further from his own.

He also knew how Christians were supposed to treat the lonely. Christians were supposed to include the outcast, and James evaluated people's Christianity by the way they treated him. By this standard, unfortunately, he met many more non-Christians than Christians. Forgiveness had no place in his personal philosophy and the more rebuffs he met, the further he withdrew from church and Christian activities. He often announced in a shaking-dust-from-the-soles way, "Don't expect me to want to become a Christian when people don't act like Christ."

True, James discriminated in his choice of Scriptural proof texts, exempting himself from responsibility for his own rude behavior—but then, after all, he was giving many folk the opportunity to offer a Christ-like welcome.

One holiday season, he called the wife of Ed Vrydoliak. Her husband, a well-known ward politician had advanced through the political machine of the senior Dick Daley and was eventually celebrated by the local media for his city council battles with Mayor Ed Washington. James angled for a holiday invitation. Mrs. Vrydoliak refused—rather diplomatically, I thought—but to James her refusal became a pretext to extend his scorn beyond middle-class Protestants to the urban Catholic community which this family represented.

I began to view James as an avenging angel, the self-ordained charity-tester of Christians throughout Chicago. I started to think, "You know, in a way he's right. Isn't there one woman's group charitable enough to include a funny man, find him a chair in the circle, and tolerate his idiosyncracies? The role of the Christian is to include the outcast in the name of Christ; to attempt to understand."

Racking my brain for Chicago contacts left over from our days in the inner city pastorate, I gave James the phone number of a Christian friend who directs a social service outreach. His defenses up, James got off the first salvo and immediately offended the secretary to such an extent that the director, my friend, told him off when she came on the line. When this was duly reported to me (first by James, then by the social services director), I thought, "I can't be the only Christian in the whole city of Chicago who can give this man an hour a week!" My ballooning pride was pricked by the ragged edge of conscience, that inner whisper so skilled at deflating pretensions. *Well, an hour a week isn't very much time to give to the loneliest man you have ever met, is it Karen?*

Right. So I made arrangements for James to visit our Chapel of the Air broadcast offices in the western suburbs. One Columbus Day, on holiday from his civil service job as a filing clerk, he took the train to our town. I met him at the station, a little gnome of a man, about five foot two, balding, in his late thirties, wearing noticeably thick glasses and a trench coat that grazed the tops of his shoes.

The way he acted kept me off-balance. He taped our conversation on his hand-held recorder, took pictures of the office workers and me, made odd little comments that could be misinterpreted because of his stutter or bluntness. We went to lunch, sitting at a table in a restaurant together. James read the menu by bending his head to the cardboard folder, and scanned the pages with his lenses nearly touching the print. I waited, noticing the waitress' glances. "We must look like beauty and the beast," I thought, pride rising.

Then the voice again, the inward prompt. *Well, since we're into fairy tales, wasn't it the beauty who kissed the beast and turned him into a handsome prince?*

I realized that my presence, my tailored and neatly coiffed presence, dignified James in the eyes of the restaurant patrons. When he scanned the menu, I smiled slightly as if to say, "This is all right. Some people have to read like this when they suffer from functional blindness." When he made strange little comments, I laughed softly, and the waitress considered him whimsical. She took him to be a droll little man, odd (which he is), but not preposterous, because he seemed to be my friend.

As we ate, I wondered: Why am I doing this? Am I spending time with him because it makes me feel better? Does this fit my image of how a good Christian woman behaves? Or worse yet, is my platform self, the one that performs in front of watching eyes—is that one making a show, a little obvious demonstration of charity?

I knew I felt pity for James's loneliness. I was just beginning to say the word myself, to open up the long vowel "o," to hiss the sibilant "s's." Still, what was this pushy sadness, this loneliness, elbowing me like an aggressive woman at the bargain counter? Loud-mouthed, she would take the best things for herself. She grabbed holidays into her shopping bag and quiet moments of reflection. L-O-N-E-L-I-N-E-S-S. I could spell the word now. But how could I possibly be lonely?

So I felt compassionate toward James, felt he needed mercy, as I was beginning to feel I did. Yet there was something else: pure oddity. James was odd, yet I was not offended, only surprised.

Looking closely, I found that my surprise was often infused with delight. The things James did, the outrageous words he spoke, amazed and delighted me. I often hung up the phone after James's litany of grievances somehow taken with the man. He had the courage, despite his psychological disabilities, to go against proprieties. He was a native iconoclast who blasted conventions. Did he say things, I, in my secret heart, wanted to say?

I felt compassionate toward James O'Brady because he was the loneliest man I knew. But I liked James O'Brady because he was odd.

Watching him eat his meal, his face so close to the plate that his nose was virtually pushing the French fries, I discovered what united us; we were, after all, two of a kind, displaced people sharing our isolation, and so, for a moment, escaping it. Even as he grilled the waitress about the ingredients of the ketchup, I thought, *On the inside, James O'Brady, I look just like you.*

Usually, when we finish our phone conversations, James often asks, still stuttering, but sometimes not so much as when we began our talks, "Well, Mrs. Mains, wh-wh-what have I done for you? Hm? Hm? N-n-any thing you have learned from me? Hm? Hm?"

One day, after months of hearing about how his latest strategy to gain entrance to a national Christian business women's organization had all to come to naught, I said, by way of answering, "James, I talked about you in a speech I gave."

Silence . . . then, "Wh-wh-what d-d-did you say?"

"Oh, I told people that you are the loneliest man I have ever met. And that you are my friend and that you know how Christians are supposed to behave. We are supposed to welcome one another as Christ has welcomed us."

James was very interested. "And wh-wh-where d-d-did you say this? H-m? H-m? I bet they were ang-ang-gry with you."

"No, they were very moved. I spoke about you to five hundred women from the Church of the Nazarene in Nashville. I told them I couldn't understand what was so wrong with a man who wanted to be part of the women's sewing circle. Women have been moving into men's clubs and business associations for the last century."

Silence on the other end of the phone.

Then James said, "Well, m-m-maybe there is a reason for all of this."

This was a lesson I knew—that God moves toward us in every human encounter—but James, my friend, the loneliest man I ever met, taught it to me again.

I am planning a Christmas celebration. This year our Christmas will not be exclusively for my children but for James O'Brady as well. We will use my mother's hand-painted Bavarian china and the silver coffee service imported from Germany. I will serve a favorite menu, roast beef and Yorkshire pudding, braised winter vegetables, and flamed plum pudding. The rooms will be lit by brass lanterns, candles, and firelight. We will hang the Christmas angels on the tree. And we will say, "For you, James O' Brady, a Christmas. Welcome here. Welcome to our home."

3

Guess Who Came to St. Patrick's Day Dinner

While vacationing in Nova Scotia, my husband's brother conducted some research into his family's genealogy and discovered that the Mains clan was Irish in its origins, rather than German as had been assumed. So mid-course in our marriage, to cultivate our sense of heritage, I decided to institute a Mains family dinner on St. Patrick's Day. The celebration that takes place in nearby Chicago — where each March 17th the city dyes the Chicago River green and holds a parade down State Street — no doubt influenced my decision. (The mayor always leads the parade and for most of my growing up years that was Richard Daley, Sr., who dressed in top hat and tails.) Certainly I, one individual, could catch the spirit of old Ireland by providing a boiled beef and vegetable dinner for my family.

Close to the third anniversary of my St. Patrick's day dinner, I received a phone call from an editor friend. She told me that Graham Kerr, once of television fame as the popular "Galloping Gourmet," was in town working on a manuscript. She thought we should meet one another: Did we have any evenings free for dinner that week?

The only night in which my husband David and I even planned to touch base was the night I had set aside for our Mains St. Pat's Day dinner. I hold to the conviction that three times around makes a tradition and was therefore reluctant to put our celebration of Irishness at risk. Why didn't she and her husband just bring Graham to our house? Then we could all tip our hat to St. Patrick together.

Now I must explain that for seventeen years or more our family lived without a television set. This peculiar renunciation places us, of course, within a miniscule percentage of the American population. Without a doubt, in looking back, this decision was one of the best we ever made for the sake of our children. Nevertheless, there was much that was good I missed. I never saw the Emmy-winning "Galloping Gourmet" series on television in the early 1970s. I had heard that Graham and his wife Treena had become Christians, left the fast-paced television industry, and were devoting their energies to the religious organization called Youth with a Mission. But not being given to celebrity-worship and without much of an impression of the man who some 200 million viewers used to watch whip up gourmet meals, I lightheartedly and without any forethought, invited "The Galloping Gourmet" to dinner.

All three boys were home. Melissa, our only daughter, was away at school on the East Coast, but Randall, our oldest, was on an odyssey between institutions of higher learning. He claimed squatter's rights to the empty bedroom, enrolled in the wonderfully cheap local junior college, and then carefully plotted his collegiate future; politics? – no; business? – no; economics? – yes! Randall (whose Gaelic name means "counseled by wolves" – apt in his case) was the child whose fourth grade teacher had called me to say, "Mrs. Mains, I'm having a little difficulty with your son. I've given all the children assignments to research and report on a foreign country. Randy has been assigned Ireland and he's resisting because he says he doesn't know how it will relate to his adult life!"

Little did my son know that he would be making cornbread for the third annual Mains family St. Patrick's Day meal in honor of our own heritage and also of our guest, the once Galloping Gourmet, Graham Kerr. Things Irish were relating to his adult life quite a bit, I would say.

I arranged the table with my everyday wedding dishes, the stylized blue and white flowers of Johnson and Johnson's "Baltic" ironstone — a set which admittedly shows the wear of the years, of constant hospitality, and of "come for supper" church work. The accessory pieces are long gone, but I have enough cups and saucers, butter dishes, and dinner plates (albeit chipped and stained) to still make up a setting for eight. I have always enjoyed the contrast of the crisp blue and white against the dark oak of the table. We boiled the brisket of corned beef, its pungent odor censing the rooms. We boiled new potatoes and carrots, added quartered onions and cabbage slices. Randall's cornbread, with chewy grains of stone-ground meal, emerged moist and fragrant from the oven.

Our guest and friends arrived. I found Graham to be handsome and warm, urbane and articulate. *This*, I thought, *could be an interesting evening.* David welcomed everyone to our home, and we recalled the funny story of his widowed Grandma Mains and her pro-German, anti-Irish biases (until World War II when, it seems, less and less was heard about Teutonic origins). We explained how we were attempting to establish a Mains family Irish tradition, and how glad we were they had come to observe it with us.

When we sat down to the table for the prayer before the meal, Graham held up his blue and white plate and said, "My grandmother brought this very pattern with her when she immigrated to the United States."

Then we brought the great ironstone platter to the table and placed it in the middle as the centerpiece of the meal. It was piled high with potatoes and bright vegetables dripping with melted butter and hedged round with the contrasting burgundy slices of beef brisket. With everything before us, our guest said, "You're not going to believe this, but this is my favorite meal. I feel right at home!"

Now I inquire: Could any third-time event, struggling for a foothold as a tradition, receive a greater endorsement?

One of our customs, when a new friend is at the table, is for the children to ask two questions which our guest must answer as honestly as possible. This custom, practiced since my children were small, has brought amazing returns. The children have developed an assured manner with adults; they've gained the capacity to make their way in social situations. (If they can just remember to ask those questions!) Just as importantly, they've heard wonderful stories, and through years of listening have stored up the rich lore of a hundred lifetimes.

Rarely are any of us given the gift of sincere interest. Something tender, something gentle happens when this gift is given. Christ comes near. How frequently did we all, family and friend alike, sense the presence of the Unseen Guest? And how frequently did we find ourselves, once strangers, now soul friends around that bargain, three-dollar-castoff, round oak dining table?

Graham Kerr rose to the occasion, gallant man that he is. He regaled the boys with stories from his life; told them how he stumbled into television over the Australian Army network when the host of a cooking show couldn't honor his commitment. Knowing nothing about cooking, but trusting his native humor and outrageous sense of fun, Kerr turned potential disaster into a hilarious media production. He was soon popular with a worldwide English-speaking audience, and gained the financial rewards that went with that kind of success.

One of the boys posed a question which is frequently asked at our table, "Well, how did you become a Christian?"

Graham then told how, at the height of his success, hotly pursuing the high life, he nevertheless faced personal, harrowing failure. His family was in distress; his wife, Treena, seriously depressed. Just before she had been scheduled to enter a psychiatric hospital, Treena finally accepted one of the many invitations their housekeeper extended to visit her church. This woman had prayed faithfully for the Kerrs through the years she had been in their employ. When Treena at last attended, she encountered the inexplicable love of God and was converted; returning home, she was not only a different woman, she was a *new* woman.

Her husband was acutely aware of the positive change in his wife, but her psychiatrist was even more so. With tears in his eyes, the phychiatrist told Graham that he didn't know what had happened to Treena, but he thought it was a miracle. All this, of course, led to Graham's own conversion.

Sitting in our dining room on St. Patrick's Day, Graham Kerr delighted my children with his tales of God's love. A story-teller, a natural *raconteur*, he was at his absolute best. We laughed, we cried, we wiped our eyes. Graham stood from his chair to get his body into the telling. I remember thinking, *Oh thank you God, that my children can hear all this, that their memory will be enriched with these marvelous tales of divine mercy.*

Well, the evening, as all good evenings must, came to an end, and we said a reluctant good-bye at the door. It is hard to become friends knowing you may never see each other again. Graham gave me a big hug and said, "Thank you for having me in your home. It's not many people who would ask me for dinner." *Only someone like me,* I thought, laughing within, *someone who doesn't know any better.*

What I do know, reflecting upon this experience, is that we are not only isolated from one another because of our oddities, but also—the world being the queer place that it is—by our giftedness. All my life I have heard variations on these phrases: "You're not like anyone I've ever known"; "I can't figure you out"; "I've never met anyone like you." One woman said to me recently, "But Karen, you're so huge!"

People have been afraid to invite David and me to dinner as well. "We wanted to have you," they say, "but you're so busy." This has contributed to my feeling of isolation.

In addition, I am coming to know that one of the things that sets me apart from others is something about myself I actually like: my uncommon attraction to the transcendent. I find a shattering meaning in the shadows cast by new spring foliage, the sunlight glistening on the sea, the wind ruffling through a shaggy field. I tip my head, perk my ear, and hear the divine incantation all around. Every moment seems spiritually pregnant. Waves on the beach call, birds cry, "God! God! God!"

I have learned that this rhythm is not a common human cadence, and whether it's a gift or a variety of soft-headedness I wouldn't want to be the one to say. I know that I have learned to be cautious when I feel exultant about the low thrumming of the spiritual I have just detected. (A friend took me aside once to explain kindly that I should be more careful when I talked about spending *hours* in prayer since no one believed me.) At any rate, whether it's James O'Brady's tactlessness, Graham Kerr's resplendent charm, or my own spiritual distraction, the strong particularities that make us who we are can also isolate us, unless someone, whether through naiveté or true generosity of spirit, is willing to meet us where we are.

I do not want ever to forget Graham Kerr's quick hug at my door, the shy words, a truth whispered, "Not many would have *me* for dinner." I do not want ever to forget that, no matter how accomplished, odd, or other-worldly, all humans need significant contact—a moment, a little while one evening, when the room bends close and love shines. I do not want to forget that the simplest thing I can say to those who pass my way is, "Come home. Come home."

25

4

A Writer Without Words

The first time I met Carolyn Martin was at the Seattle Pacific Christian Writer's Conference. Actually I heard her before I saw her. During an informal reception for the conferees, a howl emerged from somewhere in the crowded room. I heard it again, *Owu-yool-woy-ohll.* Checking to see who was in pain, I sighted a woman in a wheelchair, head, elbows and torso thrusting about in the herky-jerky dance of cerebral palsy. *Owu-yoool-woy-ohll* was her language, not a reaction to pain; these were her words.

A little later, Rose Reynoldson, the professor in charge of the conference, came to me and said that someone wanted to meet me. She led me to Carolyn Martin, the woman whose cry I had heard. Carolyn had read some of my books. So we sat together and talked.

By "talk" I mean Carolyn pecked out sentences with one finger on a small keyboard, which emitted a ticker-tape print-out, while I rushed to finish her answers, discomforted by the arduous process of her peck-lunge replies. In time, however, the bump/grind of palsy dimmed before the particular quality of Carolyn Martin's shining. By this I mean, if you were a woman without words (nothing but the unlikely facsimile of *yowl-oohl-yoh*), would you go to a writer's conference?

Carolyn gave me her work to read, and I was moved by all the beauty and pain that can compose one human being. A whole universe! A bright mind trapped in a recalcitrant body; the deprivations of forced institutionalizations; wonderful humor nevertheless; amazing nurturing love for other helpless people; and, overwhelmingly, forgiveness. I whispered to Rose, "There's a book in that woman if you can just find someone close by to help her get it out."

I went home thinking much about being a writer without words and mentioned meeting Carolyn Martin in a book of my own. Then I thought about convocations of writers. I rarely attend writers' conferences because the environment forces me to pay attention to the terror of what it means to be a writer (or perhaps what it is that I am forced to attend to is the terror of what it means for me to be a writer).

At one conference, however, I foolhardily registered with great expectations—the plenary speakers were writers I admired; and I stupidly attended without the security blanket of an accompanying friend. I had published some eight books, countless articles, and aired who-knows-how-many broadcasts, but two days going, I began to feel more and more like an aspirant without any proven talent. Sinking fast into my writer's morass of insecurities, I finally succumbed to wretchedness one afternoon; I blotted my tears with my pillow, and cocked my ear lest my roommate return and find the wreckage. Finally, I called home, desperate (like a child) for the warm, sensible voice of my husband.

No one prepares would-be writers for the agony of writing. All I ever wanted to do was put words on paper. I had no idea that my soul would also appear streaking naked. "What have I done? Have I shown more than I wanted?" The offering of these words, these passions, is no simple act; it is an intimately complex enterprise having to do with the deep hidden hopes, dreams, desires, and longings of the soul.

Writing is a matter of periodic sharp highs between many valleys of grief. Suddenly some publisher (some magazine editor) wants your work, is willing to sign a contract, print your thoughts. The euphoria you feel, that exalted joy, has little to do with the acceptance of the written piece itself, but everything (everything!) to do with all the rejections of your past, parental cursings and blessings, haunting insufficiencies, insecurities, and self-doubts. You have come home, you belong, you are wanted, someone desires you. Professional relationships are invested with impossible expectations; you speculate with adolescent grandiosity about the future.

Actually, what has happened is that a booklist has been filled, the hungry machine of some magazine editor's production schedule (so many printed pages per issue) has been fed. You become a number on an accountant's sheet, an address in a Rolodex. No one tells you that few people will remember your article. No one tells you that the average book by the average author sells a pathetic 5,000 copies. No one tells you that you are not entering into a creative marriage of souls with your editor—he is already negotiating for another job in another publishing house.

At least one-third of being a successful writer is business savvy. I was unprepared for this. No one told me I would have to know how to negotiate contracts, insist on percentage accelerators based on incremental sales, learn to read royalty statements, keep track of unintentional mistakes in different houses' accounting departments. No one told me I would have to become proficient at self-promotion. Much of this is anathema to the poetic stirrings of my creative self. I feel crushed by number crunching, disturbed by distribution patterns, maddened by business machinations.

All this creates the instability which makes writers' conferences potential sinkholes for me, and I avoid them whenever I can. I avoid them as I avoid Christian bookstores. If the stores know who I am, from having sold my other books, I'm embarrassed; and if I'm not recognized, I'm angry. And the truth is, I'm mature enough to know that I'm not mature enough, that this neurotic ambiguity is no one's fault but my own. Weeping into my pillow that miserable afternoon, I began to see that my sloppy emotions had everything to do with the loneliness I experience in being a writer.

I know that I am not the writer I could be. Improvement is near (I can touch it!). If I can just find first readers for my early manuscripts, an on-going instructive editorial relationship, a sympathetic critiquing community of mutual ability, and a creative learning environment, I can do better. (I'm not asking for much, am I folks?) Greatness is not even on my mind. I'm simply aspiring to competence. I just want to be, for the sake of my own self-esteem, as good as I can be.

No one does well in isolation. Any artist of merit has some creative community. I had come to the writer's conference expecting to make significant professional connections, and I kept sharing meals with proverbial conferees: people who compulsively register for author's seminars but never write a word for submission. Still alone creatively, my increasing need made me feel desperate.

I found myself back at the Seattle Pacific Christian Writer's Conference years later, and here I met Carolyn Martin again. She had abandoned the typewriter/printer that had once been mounted on her wheelchair. Her ability to speak had improved and she now attempted to communicate directly. She had also come along professionally as a writer. A typist/editor had been found to assist her expression. And Rose Reynoldson, that saint, had become a friend and writing mentor.

"I wrote about you!" I greeted her.

"Oa, whroo aou ooo!" (I wrote about you!) she tossed back at me, jerking her head. We laughed and smiled. I smile with my eyes and mouth. Carolyn smiles with her whole body, her grin twisting up from her toes to the tip of her head. She invited me to visit her new independent living quarters.

We joked about it. "Well, I'll come," I said, "but I hope you'll have it all cleaned for me."

I did go to her apartment. The sign on the door instructs delivery people to knock and leave their packages inside. The last words read, "I DON'T BITE!" Carolyn greets me and lets me read a note she has written prior to the conference (misspelled words are due to her bad aim):

> Rose and I are expecting to have a wonderful time this year. The speaker for the first conference that I attended was author and lecturer Karen Maimes, wife of David Maimes, speaker on the Chapel of the Air. She liked my work. Privately, she told Rose that I had the making of a book in me.

> The fun part is that Karen is going to be the keynote speaker this year. She does not know of the work I have done in these past years or that I live in my own apartment. (I lived in the group home.) This is going to be a delight to have her in my home and show her that her faith in my ability as a writer was important to me. This is where my mind and heart are now.

There was a reception in the evening at which I interviewed Carolyn Martin. I wanted the other writers to sense some of the same courage I had sensed. Rose Reynoldson acted as our interpreter.

After introducing my interviewee, I say: "Sometimes you don't speak very clearly and sometimes I don't understand you very well."

Carolyn contorts, her hands twist spastically, then flutter close to her face. It takes us awhile to work our way through this response. One almost catches Carolyn's words. I listen and repeat, searching. Rose, more adept at understanding, is nevertheless experiencing a little deafness. She listens. She repeats. We ask Carolyn to try again. This time we get it: "It's been this way all my life. But I had a choice; either I could hide myself away or I could come out and make a fool of myself—but learn."

We're relieved; the audience is relieved. Carolyn smiles, her toes and knees and elbows laugh, her hands wave near her ears. She has been understood. *Yoeah!* she says. *Yoeah!*

Then she thrusts back her head. She has something more to say. Carolyn's elbows pump inward, pumping the bellows of her lungs. The whole room is to hear this pronouncement. Her head jerks and a strangled cry tears from her, *"Ah-i-i-i-i a-a-a-a-a-m   a   wri-i-t-er!"*

And not a person of us present doesn't know the depths of this cry. And not a person of us who has made the writer's journey doesn't know that this desperate, shrieking yowl is what is necessary in order for us to continue the writer's journey. I-I-I-I-I A-A-A-M A WRITER!

And so when I fight for time, when my hours are interrupted and my quiet is stolen, when I am discontent with the writer's lot and with the soul-bruising baggage that accompanies being published, when I see the glut of books advertised in Christian periodicals and wonder what could possibly impel me to contribute to it, then I remember Carolyn Martin. I see her one finger pecking out her thoughts into the computer (the other hand holding the wrist to steady it). I see her wrenching body and hear her wrenching shout. We are sisters in the soul, she and I. Inside I twist about; my neck jerks, my knees jump, my elbows bob, and I, too, must be content to howl out meaning. But it doesn't matter. I too am a writer. And if Carolyn Martin can make the journey, so can I.

5

A Comfortably Rumpled Advocate

When people asked me what happened to our car, and when I answered that I'd had an accident and that I'd hit a police vehicle, everyone invariably laughed. "All right. All right," I wanted to say. "So I hit a police car." I didn't think the incident funny at all.

It didn't seem to matter that I was proceeding south through an intersection on the green light and that the police officer came hurrying west through it on the red. I hit him, totaled his car, and was instructed to pull into the nearest gas station parking lot while a truck towed away the wreckage. Then one of his police buddies issued me a cita-tion for failure to yield to an emergency vehicle.

How did this funny/unfunny incident happen? I don't know. All I do know is that one snowy night, I simply did not hear his siren, and I did not see his flashing lights. Two full lanes of cars on my street, which he skirted from the left, must have blocked my hearing and vision. I was told by the officer of the car I rammed that while hastening to the scene of a previous accident, just a way down the road, he had activated his emergency lights and sirens, approached the intersection with caution and adjusted the volume of the siren according to the proper legal regulations.

While I was waiting for his police department buddy to write out my ticket, another man tapped on my window. I rolled it down again. "Lady, you didn't stand a chance. That cop was parked in the line of traffic. He pulled out around stopped cars, then turned on his emergency signals. You couldn't have kept from hitting him if you tried. Me and my Dad was standing right over there." He pointed to a porch on a neighborhood bar. "We was watching the accident up the road and saw this police car and we said, 'Bet that fool cop is gonna pull out and cause a wreck.' Sure 'nuff, he did just that."

Ah, I thought, *maybe that explains why I didn't hear a siren in time.* The truth? I don't know for sure what really happened, but my insurance man thought the ticket was a little self-serving on the part of two police buddies, and he recommended that I appear in court, thinking the judge might be lenient due to poor weather conditions and bad visibility. So I decided to keep my court date.

When I appeared in traffic court, I felt as if I were participating in a minor enactment of the Great and Final Judgment. A mob of nervous, defensive people — without any common link except that they'd tangled with the traffic laws of their municipality — convened in a large room and waited in anxious awkwardness. I was amazed at the feeling of incompetence which began to smother my normal assurance. I was nervous, sweaty, and insecure as to how to proceed. Those of us ignorant in jurisprudence are defenseless before blind justice in even so small a venue as traffic court.

The bailiff entered. The clerks of the court took their places at the bench. The judge appeared; Honorable Patrick O'Shaughnessey, presiding. All in the courtroom rose. Instructions were given that all were to shout, "Here!" when their names were called, then stand in line, approach the bench in turn, declare our full names to the judge, plead whether we were guilty or not guilty, and pay our fines if guilty.

"Stacey Tucker!" called the bailiff.

A woman's voice answered, "Here!"

"David Dirkin!"

"Here!"

"Juan Morales!"

"Here!"

The line in the middle of the courtroom began to form. The judge asked questions that sorted the acquiescing offenders from those who felt unjustly accused. "Has your license ever been suspended or revoked? . . . Pay the clerk. . . . Take your seat in the courtroom."

I felt enormous compassion for those people struggling with English as a second language, and for those who were as confused by the process as I and were poor in the bargain, or who perhaps had already accumulated a series of black marks. The judge, though brusque in order to process his caseload, was also professionally kind. As I watched, fascinated now, the legal process evoked thoughts of the Last Judgment's division of the sheep from the goats. I listened to excuses and defenses and thought of that great day when all the nations would be gathered before the Great Judge.

I noticed that my policeman friend (the one whose car I had hit and whose police force buddy had given me a ticket) had now entered the courtroom. He nodded and I smiled. I wondered who the young man in a three-piece suit standing beside him was.

"Karen Mains!"

"Here!"

We both approached the bench; the policeman in his uniform, in this courthouse in *his* municipality, before the judge who had listened to *his* witness in countless other cases. I learned that the young man in the three-piece business suit beside him was an assistant district state's attorney. Suddenly the system seemed stacked against me. I had no idea the policeman would bring a lawyer with him. Ignorance ever gives permission for victimization. I did have the presence of mind to decide that if there were a chance I wasn't guilty, I did not deserve a black mark against my record in some computer file in Springfield, Illinois. I wasn't going to let the system's intimidating ways bully me into relinquishing a fair hearing. When asked how I pleaded, I stated, "Not guilty!"

Then I was informed that I could choose to have a bench trial or a jury trial. If I had had my senses about me, I would have stopped the proceedings and said, "Your honor, please explain the technicalities to me. I don't understand." Instead, I requested a trial by a jury of my peers—about that I had some comprehension.

The policeman whose car I had totaled shook his head, and I walked out of the courthouse thinking, *If my adversary is going to stand up there with an assistant district state's attorney to help him, I need to procure the services of a lawyer. Where in the world does one find a lawyer who takes care of these minor cases? And how much is it going to cost me?*

Leaving the courthouse, I noticed someone approaching me on the same sidewalk. He was a comfortably rumpled young man with a woolen winter scarf around his neck. He looked at me, looked again, and said, "Pardon me, but aren't you Karen Mains?" He explained that his children had loved one of my books — he had loved my books. We had a nice little conversation standing outside the Du Page County courthouse.

Then upon parting, he asked why I was here. I explained my dilemma and said, "You wouldn't know where I could find a lawyer, would you?"

Yes, he said. It so happened he was a lawyer, and it so happened he handled exactly those kind of cases. Needless to say, I didn't ask for his credentials. Some things are just too clear to question. I gratefully agreed to his suggestion that he help me out.

So months later, after stays and delays and rearranged court dates—and my lawyer's waiver of a jury trial for a hearing before the bench—I stood in that courtroom again. I had taken care to dress especially well. I stood opposite the policeman whose emergency vehicle I had totaled. The same nattily attired assistant district state's attorney in his three-piece, pinstriped suit and with the same air of confidence accompanied my adversary. I smiled at the policeman, I smiled and nodded to the assistant state's attorney. I particularly smiled at the judge, because this time, this time, I had a comfortably rumpled advocate.

I have rarely needed someone to defend me. I've made a point of taking care of my own problems. Something about the old female dependent role has not suited me. I have worked hard to become an independent adult, capable of functioning on my own. There is a split of sorts in my attitude toward independence, however. I know I must depend upon God, must look to him for nurture and guidance; but I don't like to depend on other people, so I have very little practice at letting someone else take over. Part of this is reactionary; often the people I have needed most have not been there when I reached out to them. In addition, I have a soft voice when I seek aid. Sometimes you have to speak up or be disappointed. The tendency for many of us when disappointed is to think, "I'll just have to learn to take care of that myself."

No matter the cause, the will to be self-sufficient developed in me, which closed me off from the gifts of the people of God. Sometimes accidents beyond our control bring home the fact that we cannot live without healthy dependencies upon others. This courtroom moment provided for me an instance of truth out of which spun larger circles of reality. The words from Scripture took on experiential meaning: "My little children, I am writing this to you so that you may not sin; but if any one does sin, we have an advocate with the Father, Jesus Christ the righteous . . ." (1 John 2:1, RSV).

The same question, "Guilty or not guilty?" was posed; the same answer, "Not guilty," was given. I carefully explained my story. The policeman explained his story. We both answered short questions from our lawyers. Then the judge said, "Oh, this is a very easy case to decide. It's clear that you are not guilty."

We walked out of the courtroom, my comfortably rumpled rescuer and me. I tried to, but I couldn't possibly express to him the depth of his gift. I had not only undergone a lesson in minor criminal proceedings, I had experienced the magnitude of what it means to have an advocate. I had found a champion, someone to stand beside me, someone to plead my cause. I had experienced the relief of trusting my incompetence to another's competence, my weakness to another's strength. What a gift in that small legal arena. And how unfathomably measurable in the spiritual realm! For a moment I had been forced to come to terms with my limits and God's care through human hands of his providing.

Carmel, my daughter-in-law to be, worked in that police department during this time as a dispatcher. After the trial, she reported overhearing my friend the policeman complaining about the results of the criminal traffic trial, "Would you believe it!" he said. "She won!" When I asked her to pull the file out of the computer to see what it said, she couldn't find it. Someone had destroyed the record. So goes the way of justice. We win and lose big battles first in minor things. But at least, due to the happenings on one snowy night, no black mark was placed against my driving record in Springfield, Illinois. All thanks to comfortably rumpled advocacy.

6

Voice on the Phone

Susan Walker and I have never met though we have talked long-distance over the phone for some five years. She lives in another state and when she first called, her son, Chris, was dying from leukemia. Phone relationships are interesting because many of the normal means of interpreting personality are not available. There is only a voice, what it says, how it sounds.

I began to realize that Susan was a desperately unhappy woman due to more than the tragedy of her son's death. Sometimes I could hear Susan's voice, in her great distress, slip into the high, frantic tones of a little child. I learned that when she was sixteen, Susan's mother had died of breast cancer; that Susan suffered from an inordinate fear of succumbing to the disease herself; that premenstrual syndrome complicated her condition; that her marriage was struggling.

At some point in this journey, I insisted that she seek professional help. I remember saying, "Susan, you just can't go through this by yourself." I feel that grief counseling should often be obtained when individuals face the death of a family member; and Susan was plagued by so many psychological

38

complications that I feared deeply for her marriage. With my encouragement, Susan found help at a mental health clinic. *And it was then that the real hell began.*

Susan fell into the hands of what I can only describe as a twisted healer, one of those professionals in the psychological field who are sick themselves, who use their knowledge to achieve power over others. To my horror, he entrapped this young woman, feeding on her most compulsive, desperate fears; and I was the party on the other end of the phone line, receiving bits and pieces of garbled information, trying to make sense out of Susan's emotional excesses, attempting to differentiate between hysteria and true victimization. I listened sometimes twice a week—two weeks might go by without any word—and then Susan would start calling again, sometimes two and three times in one day.

With horror, I realized that this counselor was manipulating Susan into abnormal attachment. He was seducing her emotionally, seducing her psychologically; he did everything but seduce her physically (and at that, only because he could not break through her strong Christian defenses). And I was helpless on my end of the phone line; there was absolutely nothing I could do.

Within a few months of her son's death, at the beginning of her hellish therapeutic journey, Susan's father died as well. Because the marriage was fragile, because the young couple was involved in ministry and quite reasonably feared broken confidences and public exposure of Susan's weaknesses, this young woman was truly alone in the world. She wandered in a maze from which she could find no exit.

Susan's calls began to come so frequently that my children would answer the phone, raise their eyebrows and say in that knowing way, their voices dropping, "Mo-om, it's Susan." Because her family income was limited, strained already due to the abnormal expenses of catastrophic illness, I deliberately limited the length of our conversations. "Now Susan, you may call me whenever you need me," I would say. "Sometimes I will be able to talk. Other times it will be inconvenient. I will tell you when it is inconvenient, but this is not because I am not here for you. I cannot promise you that I will always be here when you need me. No one can make that promise. But I will listen as much as I am able." When the phone call had lasted for fifteen minutes, I would begin to cut her off. "Now, Susan, you and Phillip (her husband) can't afford this kind of expense. We've talked for fifteen minutes, and I don't believe we should talk any more. It is time to get ready to hang up."

Arm-chair psychologist that I am (the most dangerous kind, I know), I diagnosed Susan's problem as an obsessive/compulsive disorder. I am not given much to compulsion or obsession, but I became intimately familiar with both during this phone acquaintance. Susan had a deep-seated, uncontrollable fear of abandonment. This left her abnormally vulnerable to manipulation and abuse; she would attach to male authority figures like the proverbial puppy that sinks its teeth into a pant leg and will not let loose—though shaken, though pulled, though beaten.

There was what I might call a "narcissistic howl" in Susan. A great wail went up out of her wounded child-self, which I can only compare to my six-month-old firstborn who screamed uncontrollably when I left him in the church nursery and who would not be appeased by anything but my physical presence. Any hint of abandonment, when her therapist would set limits, when he would hang up on her desperate phone calls, and Susan would revert to a child-self controlled by fear and anxiety. She would even refer to herself in the third person, "He's cruel to Susan. Susan doesn't like to be treated that way."

Lest I paint myself as a heroine, let me confess that, like my children, I often raised my eyebrows in desperation. I gave counsel as I listened to endless, redundant phone conversations; over and over we tracked the same territory. I quoted Scripture. I prayed over the phone. I took Susan through healing-of-the-memory prayers. We found her child-self and attempted to create secure imaginative environments. One terrible night, we worked our way through a suicidal landscape.

Susan knew she was obsessively attached to this twisted healer, but she couldn't separate from him. She needed him, she wanted him, he had power over her. I could be nothing but the voice on the other end of the phone line saying: "I'm here Susan. I love you. I'm praying for you."

Her desperation went on for four years. Not that there weren't good moments, moments of strength and improvement when Susan would find the courage to begin detaching; but the instant she separated even slightly, her therapist would yank her back into bondage in deviously clever ways. And Susan's frantic self would run back, sink her teeth into his pant leg, and plead, "No, no! Don't leave me! Don't leave me!"

A thousand times I thought: *I have to accept the fact that some people are so damaged they cannot heal.* The world is full of maimed strays (for whom I have a particular affinity). Listening over and over, I reminded myself: *I have to come to the conclusion that we don't understand enough to treat everyone.* A thousand times, I gave up on Susan. But some inner necessity compelled me. How could I abandon one who struggled so against her own obsessions?

She cried out to God, she pled for his help. She took her Bible into her therapy session, placing it as protection on the psychologist's desk. Everything I suggested, she tried. This thrusting about, this messy determination, this great wail for health, for deliverance, deserved some kind of advocacy. If I could be nothing more than a voice at the other end of the phone, then by God's help, I could at least be that.

In one chilling moment, I also realized that if she ever appealed for outside intervention, this professional charlatan could justify any of his unorthodox approaches. (He actually triangulated the relationship by bringing his wife, also a counselor, into the crisis. She became jealous of Susan; Susan was threatened by her relationship to her husband. I believe the man took delight in this agony.) He could simply say his client was out of touch with reality, which was true!

I realize I also have portrayed this young woman at her most vulnerable; but she is, despite the agony we shared, also most lovable. I enjoy Susan's gift of original analogy. I wish in the hours of phone conversation I had jotted down her many creative expressions. Often a surprising turn of phrase would leave me delighted. Once she said that leaving her therapist would be like taking the hook from a fish's mouth and tearing the whole stomach and gut out along with it. Once in describing her irrational anxieties, she said, "I need to remind myself that these fears are not real. They're just like the ghost house at Halloween. The rooms were dark, and they put my hands into squishy plates and something terrible bumped in the dark and someone screamed. But when the lights were turned on, I could see it was only a cardboard box and plates with skinned grapes or cold spaghetti and my brother in a monster costume making weird noises. That's all these things are that frighten me. When the light is up, when God is smiling, there's nothing to be afraid of."

Finally, to my amazement, Susan gathered enough health to attempt to stand on her own. She cancelled an appointment; she asked for a break of two weeks. Instead of saying, "Hurrah!" her counselor punished her by refusing her access to another appointment, evoking—as he knew it would—her terror of abandonment.

But this time he got more than he bargained for. She went out of control in his office. He notified the police, who admitted her, in wrist and leg cuffs, to the psychiatric ward of the local hospital. She called me from that floor. After four years of bondage in a psychological hell, victim to a tormenter sicker than herself, Susan had finally escaped.

She was assigned to the care of a true healer, a psychiatrist good, kind, and wise. And whereas I had previously been intimate to the workings of true evil, to entrapment, I now became listening witness to intervention, to protection for the wounded.

Within weeks of her hospitalization, Susan's phone calls came less frequently. Now, only every once in a while do I hear a voice, wavering on the other end of the line. "Karen?" it questions—meaning, are you there?

Recently, Susan called and said, "Oh, I'm doing so well. I'm finishing my master's degree in psychology. I just wanted to tell you I'm okay and to thank you. I can't believe what I put you-through."

I am just beginning to understand myself what Susan "put me through," or did for me. I'm seeing why I stayed on the line. At the time of our phone friendship, a wail was also opening up in me. In my own way, I knew Susan's desperation at not being able to make significant human connections. (I just knew it more quietly.) I understood her relief at knowing there was a voice at the other end of the phone, one soft and gentle and yet able to laugh at human foibles. "I am here, Susan," were the words I spoke, a whisper close and calm. "I am here," were the words I, too, needed spoken.

One Mother's Day during that time, I spent the afternoon in my bedroom, weeping, alone. This is silly, I thought, why am I hurting? I had never required attention on special days before. My daughter, Melissa, had sent a plant, but none of the boys—worst of all, not even my husband, David—had remembered me.

When I questioned my husband about this shortcoming (after the tears were past), he responded by saying, "But you're not my mother!"

"I'm your children's mother!" I tossed back. "You should remind the boys."

Things might have been better if I had had my own mother to honor that day. But she had died two years before. Visits with my maternal grandmother—who had once been a comforting presence in my life—now only reminded me that she was aged and grieving for the loss of her child. She needed my laughter. "Oh, Karen, it is always so wonderful to hear you laugh!" And so I dragged joy from my soul, whenever I could, so we could laugh together, loudly, in deference to her deafness. But the female lineage in my family was tearing, gone and going. I could not reach out and hold their dear flesh. I, too, needed a woman's voice, soft and gentle, saying, "I'm here. I'm here."

Just then, in a terrible irony, my friends seemed to be needing *me* more than ever. My spiritual mentor had suddenly turned to me for solace. A friend of some twenty years began to reveal her long struggle against suicide. Two close acquaintances were suddenly overwhelmed by the truth of repressed memories which confronted them with the horrific scenes of their sexual abuse as children. Together, a neighbor and I watched her husband's life being swallowed by cancer, and we considered her approaching widowhood.

Gathering up my own pain and looking to share it with others, I found that everyone was overburdened with care already; in comparison to their distress, my pain, my loneliness, appeared less urgent. I attempted to forget its weight.

So I, too (without knowing it), needed a voice close, as close as my ear. And I heard Susan's wail, her lonely shriek from her child-self, inordinate to be sure, often out of control, but familiar; oh, so familiar. And I said the words, "I am here," and in saying the words to her, I unconsciously said them to myself. I am here. You will get well. This pain will pass. Health is near. You are not alone.

This is Susan's great gift to me. My own words from my lonely heart flew to her need; then came back again, nesting at home. The gifts of strangers are strange indeed. In the future, I will listen closely to the messages strangers evoke from me.

PART III

Travels with Strangers

7

People You Meet on Texas Back Roads

Often as I travel, I have cause to remind myself (sometimes through clenched teeth) that God is in control. The sovereignty of God's planning in my life became apparent with startling clarity two weeks after my mother's death.

Scheduled to speak at a women's retreat in Glen Eyrie, Colorado, I thought about cancelling due to my shock at her sudden heart attack and my emotional depletion from going through a family funeral, but I decided to honor my contract instead.

I had been assigned one of the turret rooms in the castle-like headquarters at Glen Eyrie. I immediately opened the curtains, as is my custom. I hate to sleep in curtained rooms. I want to look up and see the night sky, watch the moon as it passes overhead, anticipate the coming morning, and then wake in the pale light of dawn to a new day.

In this room, the windows were like a latticework, extending from waist-level up some twenty feet, their spiked arches peaking just underneath the two-story-high ceiling. They opened out onto a vista of red rock formations, like those which make up the nearby Garden of the Gods. I rested in that beauty, and in between my speaking assignments, I curled up in bed to watch the progress of those three days. Surrounded by peace, by the substantial safety of the room's stone walls, I thought: *Two years ago when I accepted these meetings, God knew I would need this room and this light and this view of the mountains. He knew that I would come here fragile with mourning. He planned this hiatus, this time when considerate women let me slip away, let me climb the stairs, crawl into bed, where I can be still and where no one will bother me.*

Whenever untoward circumstances happen, I remind myself of what I know but sometimes forget by saying, "God is in control; God is in control."

The control God exercises somehow takes into account human chaos and turns it to his own purposes. This was true in the instance of my grieving for my mother—about which I will say more later. This was also true in a more comic way during an episode from last fall's travel schedule.

I was speaking at a retreat in Texas. My plane took off after a delayed departure from O'Hare airport and arrived too late for me to catch the commuter that was to take me to my final destination: Tyler, Texas. No problem here: missed connections are a common part of my travel experience. I called the conference center where I was due to speak that evening and the director suggested that I rent a car and set off on the hour and a half drive to ensure that I would make it on time.

Now a problem presented itself. One of my children had borrowed my charge card and hadn't replaced it in my wallet.

It is difficult, to say the least, to rent a car with only a smile and earnest promises. I was still unruffled, however, because another couple had missed the same commuter flight and were also deciding how to proceed to their final destination (which happened to be along the same route). At this point, I began to exercise a modicum of faith. (God is in control, remember?)

The husband wore a cowboy hat, cowboy boots, jeans, and a gold chain. His wife carried a new mink coat. She and I discussed the complicated negotiations while waiting for our luggage. Biff, the husband, chain-smoked and kept his nose in a paperback novel. But eventually, he and I went to rent a car (while his wife watched their luggage), and we used Biff's charge card, Biff's driver's license, and, eventually, Biff's knowledge of Texas highways to get where we were going.

Mine was a sophisticated hitchhiking maneuver if there ever was one — no need to stand on the highway with my thumb out. And so far I had behaved maturely: I had not become rattled about the missed connection, or about my borrowed charge card, or about this excursion into the gathering night with total strangers. (Biff happened to be a surgeon, a member of the Presbyterian church, and a man who eagerly shared his experiences as a volunteer medical missionary. Never judge a man by his cigarette, cowboy boots, gold chain, and paperback novel.)

My rescuers made arrangements for her mother to pick them up at a McDonald's outside of Tyler, Texas; then they proceeded to their destination, kindly leaving the rental car (in Dr. Biff's name) with me.

Here I confess to flurries of panic while wandering around on dark country back roads. I have some night blindness and the signs were often illegible to me in the shadows. Furthermore, I was supposed to turn right on Pine Cove Road, but the sign at the "fourth street from the shopping center" read Lake Placid Road. Passing the marker five or six times with my headlights catching the faded letters (Yep! Still Lake Placid Road), I wandered with mounting frustration up and down the highway as the clock on the dashboard warned me that I was getting perilously close to my speaking time — 9:15 p.m.

Several inquiries helped me identify the right approach. Dumb me! — locals knew that Pine Cove Road was marked Lake Placid Road at this end. I stepped, almost literally, from the parking lot onto the platform. Everyone was relieved to see me, as I was relieved to be seen, but my first words as I walked onto the platform were: "I hope you like my outfit, because you may be seeing it for the next three days." As grown up as I had been so far (with a little bit of wobbling on dark, strange roads), I was to be put to the supreme test. My suitcase had been lost in Dallas. And not one airline employee knew where it was.

I spoke that evening, as planned, on growing up spiritually, hearing myself make remarks that had an all-too-immediate personal application. And I went to bed feeling like a little girl in a strange place, knowing I would have to wear the same travel clothes I had worn on the airplane (and which I had happened to wear for the two days of meetings which preceded my trip to Texas). The thought was not appealing; but I reasoned with myself, "Okay, Mains. You've just challenged these women to spiritual maturity. You've been a good sport up to this point and God has taken care of you. You're feeling low because you're travel-weary and tired of coping. You've been in bed this week with a low-grade virus, and you don't have the comfort of fresh, familiar clothes in the morning. Now, what does Christ think about this? How would he want you to behave? How would he behave in similar circumstances?"

These are the wrong questions to ask if one is prone to self-pity.

I remembered immediately that Christ sent out his disciples with no money in their purses, no spare sandals, and no extra luggage. I clearly recalled the Scripture written to Timothy, "Take heed to yourself and to your teaching . . . " (1 Timothy 4:16, RSV). (From where do these verses pop up when I most want to avoid their cold comfort?) I decided, as I tossed in my strange bed in my strange room in sleeping quarters on a campground I hadn't even seen because of nightfall, that I had better grow up. As always, despite the circumstances, Christ expected me to model authenticity in what I was teaching, to exhibit an emotional and spiritual maturity that testified to the reality that God was in all of life, the good and the bad.

I reminded myself of how I had experienced God's love in these last confusing moments. I had been well enough to make the journey after my bout with the flu. The couple at the airport had taken me with them when I could have been stranded without my charge card. And my carry-on case had everything I really needed: toiletries, my Bible and speaking notes, and a jogging suit for sleeping. I had even slipped in a pair of low-heeled shoes, something unusual for me when packing; I wouldn't be forced to spend the next two days tromping around the conference center in dress heels.

All was well. I woke the next morning with a sportsmanlike attitude, and the first words I uttered when I began to speak on a favorite topic, "The God Hunt: The Discipline of Finding God in All of Life," were, "No, my luggage hasn't come. But I discovered I did have a change of clothes. I am wearing my pajama tops!"

At the announcement that I was wearing my pajama tops—the shirt of a warm, blue sweatsuit—the women laughed. They all leaned toward me. My acceptance of the situation created an instant rapport, enabling my teaching ministry to work deeply. Grow up, I taught; be big girls now. Unintentionally, I had become the living model of everything I was saying.

My suitcase arrived later, and it was wonderful to have that change of clothes, but I was prepared to be a big girl without them, not to fuss or whine or feel sorry for myself.

When children attain a new level of development, parents are wise if they will affirm this with hurrahs and cheers and warm words of approval. All of us have seen daddies and mommies clap wildly when their little toddler takes his first teetering steps. This is called positive behavior reinforcement. The women in Pine Cove Conference Center didn't know it, but they affirmed my growth steps.

On the morning of my last speaking assignment, I was a little late for the meeting because I was chatting with a new friend over breakfast. Thinking about packing and getting ready to drive Biff's rental car back to the Dallas airport, I walked into the meeting during a time of hymn singing, which stopped abruptly, as if on cue. The women rose to greet me, to say good-bye. Over their street clothes, they were all wearing pajama tops, night gowns, or robes.

This was like having a room filled with some two-hundred-and-fifty mommies; some grey-haired, some with shiny blond tresses, some with curly perms—but all standing beside me and cheering. "Hey, we knew you could do it! What a big girl! What a big, big girl!"

I had come to teach them how to grow up spiritually, and they were the ones who applauded my own faltering steps into maturity. We can only laugh at our own pretensions, we speakers, and stand humble before the fact that one never knows whom one will meet, or what one will find, or what one will learn on Texas back roads.

8

The Morning Hymn Singers

While reading the romantic novel, *Romona,* a popular tale written in the late 1800s by Helen Hunt Jackson about prejudice and injustice in the American Southwest, I was struck by a passage that described the morning custom of a devout Mexican family:

> ... As the first ray reached the window, he would throw the casement wide open, and standing there with bared head, strike up the melody of the sunrise hymn.... At the first dawn of light, the oldest member of the family arose, and began singing some hymn familiar to the household. It was the duty of each person hearing it to immediately rise, or at least sit up in bed, and join in singing, and the joyous sounds pouring out of the house were like the music of the birds in the fields at dawn. The hymns were usually invocations . . . and the melodies were sweet and simple.

Ever since reading this, I have wanted to be a part of a household that lifts its voices in a morning hymn. I hold an idealized vision of that Mexican hacienda, the verandas, the gardens, the tile-lined patios, the desert roses in clay pots.

I see daylight chasing receding shadows. I hear a sonorous note raised in praise; hear sleepy voices joining softly, then robustly, in the hymn. A little farther off, bells toll from a mission church; they, too, ring out alleluia. What a wonderful way to begin the day, I think, and how impossible in my twentieth-century, contemporary, all-too-busy American family.

I am a morning person and I love to watch the rising light. In late spring after the weather warms and in the summer months, I take my coffee cup into the screened-in porch at dawn. There I sit with my Bible and journals, organizing my responsibilities, and I watch the sun rise, its golden beams slanting through the woods. The birds and I strike up our morning hymn—the great anthem of the world, its gratitude for this pure moment. But no other human voice sings the hymn with me. I am alone in my glad greeting of the day.

The singing of a morning hymn turned out to be a gift given to me by a group of women God used to teach me a hard lesson. I lived with a committee of retreat planners for a week. I had been invited to speak at their back-to-back conferences in California. Three hundred conferees came for the first three-day retreat. A twenty-four-hour break followed, after which the second group of six hundred arrived.

A speaker, such as myself, never knows what mortifications she may endure on her travels. Young women, their eyes bright and eager, sidle close to me after a meeting and say, "I would love to do what you do. I would love to travel and speak publicly." They have no idea what they are asking for. Paul said, "For this gospel I was appointed a preacher and apostle and teacher, and therefore I *suffer* [italics mine] as I do" (2 Timothy 1:11-12, RSV). God takes seriously the role of his public servants. James, the apostle, explains: "Let not many of you become teachers, my brethren, for you know that we who teach shall be judged with greater strictness" (James 3:1, RSV). Humility and authenticity are downright painful lessons to learn, and some who should learn these lessons never do.

54

The week before I left for the California retreat, I contracted an Asian flu. After spending several miserable days in bed, my health partially returned. In its midwestern grand tour, this virus had taken many people down a second time with relapses. I could feel my physical condition wavering. To complicate things, word had come that our two college-age children had collaborated on a one-act play, which was to be mounted as a student production in the theatre department of Miami University in Ohio. The temptation was very strong to cancel my commitment. I had every legitimate reason to stay home due to illness, then on the weekend I could delight in my children's creation by traveling to Oxford, Ohio, with David.

Because I plan my speaking schedule two years in advance, I must trust to the principle of divine sovereignty. In fifteen years, I have only missed three meetings — two when O'Hare airport was closed down due to weather conditions, and one because of debilitating illness. And even in these negative situations, God had turned my adverse circumstances to good account. Once after I cancelled due to the airport's closing, a woman from West Point called me and reported: "We had the best retreat ever." They had used a local speaker in my place and had spent more time in small groups. So I don't fret if I can't make a commitment; but I do attempt at all costs to honor my contracts if I am able. God has a plan. I felt it would be extremely difficult for the upcoming California double-conference to procure another speaker for six days on such short notice. Hopefully, I would mend along the way.

Dragging myself to church Sunday morning in order to take communion, I grabbed a fistful of my pastor's robe and hurriedly whispered, "I'm going to need you to pray for me." After the worship service, he met me at the communion rail, and anointed me with oil, praying for my health. I am always strengthened by these holy ministrations given through human means, but this Sunday, in an unusual way, I immediately felt an enveloping warmth, the mysterious embrace of the supernatural. I went home and slept deeply all afternoon. In the evening, I packed my clothes and notes, and departed the next day for California.

Members of the coordinating committee met me at the airport. I told them about being ill. Asking their pardon, I explained that except when I was to speak I felt it would be wisest for me to hide myself in my room and sleep.

Trying not to make too much fuss, I plotted a course for the next two days that took me to the tabernacle for the meeting, to the platform, and back to my room, then again the tabernacle, to the platform, and back to my room. In between, I rested and was deeply grateful that I was able to deliver my first speeches without interruptions due to coughing fits.

In the quiet of those days, I also had time to consider what a precious gift had been given to me in my new pastor at home. Those of us in ministry are rarely the recipients of ministry ourselves. After having been a pastor's wife, I had now become the recipient of what my husband had given to so many others—the tender, gentle support of pastoral care. What's more, my pastor was an Episcopalian of strong evangelical convictions. Wasn't this amazing? A clergyman from one denomination had prayed for me so that I, a woman alone, could minister to another portion of Christ's body. I was truly learning about the unity and diversity of the church universal.

At my first speaking session, groggy with antihistamines, weak-kneed but grateful for strength enough to stand and teach, I mentioned what a help my rector had been. "Isn't God's body wonderful?" I exclaimed to the conferees.

Some of my hearers didn't think so. They heard Episcopalian and little else. To them, from that moment on, my words were suspect.

Later, not being up to form, I committed a real mistake. Teaching on forgiveness, I explained how I had benefitted from confessing my sins following the Episcopal Church's Rite of the Reconciling Sinner. It provides a means that stands between the abused ritual of Catholic confession and the nonexistence of public confession in evangelicalism. I feel this form is one of the ways the church can work out its obedience to the Scriptural passage from James that instructs us to "confess our sins to one another." Unfortunately, I did not make the theology behind the rite clear enough—that I was not confessing to a man but to God in the presence of a witness.

Consequently, I was taken to task. A younger woman, twenty years my junior, whose husband had just graduated from seminary, took it upon herself to visit me in my sick room and examine my doctrine. Did I believe that Christ was the mediator between God and man?

I resisted the temptation to begin my reply with the condescending phrase, "My dear young woman...." She also took that opportunity to inform me that when I had been unable to accept an invitation to speak to her group of seminary wives, someone had said: "That's probably just as well. I really don't know about Karen Mains's doctrine." (Probably because I had written a book on the Holy Spirit.) At this point such inquisitors often begin to compare you to the other speakers they wish had been available.

I suddenly realized I was being thrust into a drama overloaded with psychic intensities. I dared not give way to the anger, the feelings of effrontery welling up in me. That outrage could undo my recuperation. Paul's clear instructions to the young Timothy gave check to my tongue. "And the Lord's servant must not be quarrelsome but kindly to everyone, an apt teacher, forbearing, correcting his opponent with gentleness" (2 Timothy 2:24, RSV).

I struggled instead to find compassion for this young woman. Her husband and she had just been deputized as missionaries to Europe. And suddenly, understanding, I detected those all-too familiar pretensions of one's early public life. She had recently come back from her deputation meetings; all eyes had been turned toward the young couple. She had probably been fed, feted, and asked for advice. She considered herself a teacher with much to give the church of Europe. I wanted to ask her how she would behave when a young woman, some twenty years later, came to her and examined her doctrine (because, if she stays in public ministry, this will happen). All I can hope is that I gave her a decent model as to how to cope.

She did me a great favor, however; she prepared me for the visitation of the retreat committee. They, too, had heard complaints, and several of them, in their official capacity, visited me in my bed chamber and kindly (some with detectable embarrassment) voiced their concerns, listened to my explanations, and received my apologies.

I truly felt saddened by the need for their corrections. I am a professional communicator. Our broadcast airs over 500 outlets, with a listernership that totals in the millions and includes every possible denomination. I cannot afford to forget that some religious groups are like closed family systems which only feel comfortable with habitual means of expression: the same words, the same gestures. Many of these folk live in a church house with sealed windows. All winds that force thinking—doubt, questions, new ideas, heated open discussion—are feared. If I wanted to consider myself a gifted communicator, I had to remember to frame my sound content in a way that did not offend. That was my job.

Furthermore, I had to keep a watch on my own pretensions. Had I slipped into thinking that since I was a well-known Christian writer and speaker I was entitled to certain privileges? Had I forgotten that I was a servant to all those with whom I worked? Could I accept chastisement in a Christ-like way? Could I deny myself the luxury of self-defense? "My word!" I wanted to say. "I've come all this way sick and needy. I'm missing an important family gathering. My doctrine is evangelically sound." But then, did I really believe that we who teach shall be judged with greater strictness because we have greater responsibilities? (Beware, young woman with bright and eager eyes, these questions are not easy ones to answer in practice.)

During the twenty-four-hour break between conferences, the committee and I mended our awkward relationship. When I mentioned to the committee that I had always wanted to sing a morning hymn, telling them the story from *Romona*, the women responded.

Before breakfast, each remaining day of the conference, we gathered together in the hallway of our hotel and sang the praise chorus, "I love you, Lord." One voice would begin to sing alone, calling us to the Lord's praise. Then women opened their doors—toothbrushes, curling irons, blow dryers in hand. Harmony and pitches were struck and we stood (in various stages of dress and undress) lifting our voices. "And I lift my voice to worship you. . . ."[1] For me this was an ideal finally realized and a lovely gift—but the Lord was not done with me yet.

During the second conference, I rephrased my inappropriate expressions, and after teaching on forgiveness this time, women stood in line for close to an hour to take advantage of the offer I had made to pray with them. Without the honing worked by the prior conflicts, a new clarity in my communication would not have given these women permission to divest themselves of old and terrible griefs.

The leadership committee had indeed taught me something—an important lesson: Teachers must minister as servants. Every circumstance, good or bad, is given for us to model Christ-likeness. We serve the moment. We serve Christ in the moment. We also serve the people who meet us there.

---

1. "I Love You Lord," by Laurie Klein. Copyright 1978, 1980 House of Mercy, admin. by Maranatha! Music.

So now every time I hear the phrase, "I love you Lord, and I lift my voice . . . ," I think about this retreat. I see my morning companions singing our morning hymn. Often when I am alone, drinking my coffee, watching day come, I hear these women's voices, hear the melody line, the harmony. And I never think of them without love, without sisterliness.

9

The Women's Circle

Writer Maxine Hancock, whom I had never met, phoned me from Canada. "Karen, are you going to do a book on child sexual abuse? Because if you don't, someone needs to." All of those traveling in women's ministries, like Maxine and me, had become aware of the high incidence of child sexual abuse in the background of the women to whom we were ministering. We were like itinerant priests — here today, gone tomorrow — to whom people gave the deep secrets they could not give to others.

I told Maxine, "No, I don't plan to." I had recently finished two weeks of broadcasting on the topic, which resulted in literally hundreds of letters from abuse survivors. This had necessitated that our staff counselor and I write back volumes of correspondence. In addition, in order to be accurate as a communicator, I had already spent five months in intensive research. The literature on child sexual abuse makes horrific reading, to say the least, even when the stories recounted are washed through the technical terminology of the sociologist. Enough was enough. For my own emotional and psychological well-being, I wanted some distance from this grave societal problem.

In the middle of the night, however, I realized my research brought with it responsibilities. I had become aware of profound pain. Often knowledge demands further action. Because Maxine and I were advocates for those survivors who could not be advocates for themselves, I called Maxine back. If she would co-author the project, then I felt I could give another six months to this dreaded work. She was right. Someone needed to do something for the sake of those who suffered.

The writing of *Child Sexual Abuse: A Hope for Healing* (Harold Shaw Press) wrought a surprising spiritual change within me. This is often the case with writers. We write about topics in a way that leads us to deeper truths about ourselves.

Part of Maxine's co-authoring responsibility was to provide case studies of those who had been involved in child sexual abuse (CSA). Conducting interviews, she framed four studies which were exemplary in their depiction of the profound damage incurred by this aberrant behavior.

When I read Kathy's story (one of the four), portions seemed familiar. Then I remembered a letter that had come my way after a speaking engagement in Hamilton, Ontario. And I also remembered how reluctantly I had dragged myself away from family, work, hearth, and hearthside in order to spend that weekend in Canada. "Wheels within wheels," I thought as I remembered Kathy. Hers had been one of hundreds of survivors' voices which had impelled me to collaborate on this book. But let me quote from Kathy's own words:

> My childhood was very normal until I was about five years of age. Beginning at the age of five and continuing until I was almost twelve, I was sexually abused by an uncle who lived close by, who was almost like a big brother to me. He was nineteen when it started. . . . [1]

---

1. From *Child Sexual Abuse: A Hope for Healing*, copyright 1987 by Maxine Hancock and Karen Mains. Used by permission of Harold Shaw Publishers, Wheaton, IL.

Kathy goes on to write about her misery as an adult, married and mothering her own children:

As the pressures increased with two small children, it became more and more difficult to cope with what I was feeling. The summer I was expecting our third child, I reached a new low. Once again I became suicidal. Every day I would think of ways to kill myself—and then I would check myself, feeling that it would be unfair to leave my husband with two babies. Then I would think that maybe I should kill all three of us and leave my husband free. Time after time I would put the two little boys in the car and drive at absolutely crazy speeds, hoping that we would all be killed.

One morning during that summer when I was pregnant with our daughter, I woke up with an overwhelming desire to die. I dressed the two boys and went out to the car again. This time, I thought, I would drive the car off a cliff. But again, as I drove toward my destination, I felt, "Oh, I can't do this!"

Crying and desperate . . . I knew that somehow I had to get help. I had to let somebody know what was going on inside me. I drove the car to the plaza, went into a department store, and began to steal as much as I could shove into my purse. In my distraught condition, I reasoned that if I did something bizarre enough—like shoplifting when I had lots of money in my purse and every credit card you could ask for—I would get help. The court, I thought, would surely appoint a psychiatrist.

But what happened was both more and less than what I had expected. As I left the store, I was apprehended by a security guard and taken back into the store while the police were called. Then I was taken to the police station and put into a holding cell—I and my two little boys. I was charged, finger-printed, and finally released. When my court appearance came, I went to court alone, refusing to get a lawyer. I just wanted to be punished—and perhaps, helped.

But as it turned out, the court could not have cared less about me as a person. Not a single question was asked. I was declared guilty as charged. I paid the fine and was released, worse off than I had been before. I had only added guilt to guilt.

Working with this story, typing Kathy's pain into my computer, I kept thinking, *If ever there were a picture of a soul in hell, this is it.* Kathy's self-image, her sexual image, had been shattered by early seduction and continued abuse. She was tortured by false guilt (having taken on her victimizer's true guilt), and now the guilt of her own errors complicated her agony. One simply could not be a dispassionate reporter, sitting at one's desk. As I read Kathy's words, I was drawn again into the pathos, the rage, the helplessness, the horror of this trauma. I hurt again, as I had for months, with all those bearing the wounds of child sexual abuse.

Kathy was not a Christian. She tells about being invited to a conference where I was the speaker.

I really didn't want to go. I didn't think I could stand a whole day of religion. But I ended up going. . . .

The conference I attended was the turning point of my life. . . . As Karen started talking about how our subconscious minds deal with guilt, I suddenly felt as though she was describing me—from the inside out. She explained that our subconscious mind suppresses guilt, pushing it down until finally it surfaces in various ways: in erratic behavior, in anger, in depression. I knew all too well everything she was describing.

At the end of the session, Karen had everybody close their eyes. . . . "Now if someone else has hurt you, I want you to ask God for strength to forgive that person."

I sat there, stunned. I couldn't believe what she was saying. I thought, "She can't mean this. She can't be asking me to forgive my uncle." She kept talking about giving our past with all of its pain to Jesus, and asking him to help us forgive that individual who had hurt us.

My fists were clenched, and I was actually gritting my teeth. I was desperately torn. But finally, reluctantly, needing God's forgiveness too much myself to hold onto this pain, I said, "OK, then. Lord, I'm willing to forgive."

It was a most reluctant obedience, but God honored it. It was as much as I was able to do at the time. I'll never forget that second for as long as I live. There I sat in a room with six or seven hundred other women, and I felt like I was alone with God. From the bottom of my feet up through my whole body a great weight simply disappeared.

The feeling was almost indescribably like a cool, clean breeze blowing through me. And I knew that something had happened in that moment of forgiveness. . . . When I got home, my husband was shoveling the driveway. I said to him, "My life's never going to be the same from this day on. I don't know what has happened, and I can't explain it, but I'm sure things are going to be different."

When I read these words, I wept. I am weeping now. Public ministry is hard on me. Without being self-serving, I often suffer when I am ministering in retreats. Some people thrive on public roles. They are constitutionally fit for it! My constitution requires the prayer closet, a nearby community of trust and intimacy, long walks in solitude. Public ministry throws me into an existential dither. That inward word came to my heart as I considered Kathy's freedom, *Wouldn't it have all been worth it, Karen, if there had only been this one?*

Tears running, sniffling, grabbing for tissues, I nodded. I had gone to so many places slowly, slowly. I hated the home-leaving, the interrupted work, the absence from my children's activities. I detested the tendency toward celebrity worship in the contemporary church. But if there had only been this one, this Kathy, desperate for help, with her soul delivered from an earthly hell . . . yes, yes, it would all have been worth it. Then the whisper again, the inward nudge, *But there have been hundreds, most of whom you will never know.*

I had sinned. I knew it as I sat at the computer, blowing my nose, staring out the window. God had given me a task and I had done it, but reluctantly, most reluctantly. Working with Kathy's story, my soul was stripped bare before my Lord. I saw that I should have responded all along: "Thank you for seeing fit to use me in any way you choose! I have never felt so ashamed."

Desperate new truth demands commensurate action. I took myself to my pastor and asked if he would be the human witness as I confessed my error aloud to God. I believe that Christ is the mediator between God and man, but the apostle James teaches that there are times when we must make public confession. The healthy humiliation worked by this act of repentance was exceedingly fruitful.

Then I asked my pastor to hear me make a series of vows. They indicated the seriousness of my intent.

"I vow I will no longer hide when You ask me to step into the public. I vow that to the best of my ability my life will be the living out of the prayer, 'Yes God, and again Yes, and Yes again.' I vow that I will not complain about itinerant ministry, but will fast and pray before each meeting and will attempt to consider it the awesome privilege that it truly is."

This is a remarkable communion we are part of, is it not? God uses me, a recalcitrant, foot-dragging itinerant teacher, to bring His profound freedom into the life of a woman tormented by her past. Then He uses that woman to bring humility to me because of my half-hearted obedience. Then another woman (Maxine) reminds me of my responsibility to Christ's larger body. Then He uses us all to share His grace with thousands of others who read our words, and He uses those to help who knows how many others. Wheels within wheels. Or in this case, circles — women's circles, interlocked, connecting, moving each other along.

What writer Charles Williams called the spiritual principle of "coinherence" teaches that we are a small part of a larger whole. What little I do is a partial contribution that is not complete without the contributions of others. There are, of course, many who can do this work as well as I. And I need to make war against the false pride that leads me to self-importance. I am a giver of God's gifts, but also a receiver from others of His gifts to me. I cannot do the work of God alone; nor do I need to. God forgive me if ever in the secret arrogance of my heart I thought it was so.

10

Angels on My Way Home

The flight home from any meeting where I have been speaking can be a long and lonely journey. I have expended myself utterly. I have rooted my soul in the souls of new friends, from whom I am now being parted and whom I will most likely never see again. I have entered into a period of intense concentration, noted body language, interpreted nuances of tone, drawn hurting folk close for prayer. And often, some sort of corporate love relationship has been established, a nuptial agreement between strangers' hearts. Going home, tearing myself from all this bonding, is a lonely business.

I had been in Cannon Beach, Oregon, for six days. For the first three days I worked on a book, putting in long hours entering new material into my Macintosh Computer — fifteen not-very-portable pounds I had transported with me from Chicago. Nevertheless, I thought I had preserved enough energy for the weekend retreat that followed at the Cannon Beach Conference Center.

The Lord worked in all our lives during that weekend; but on the ride over the mountain to the Portland airport in order to catch my plane, I realized I was deeply tired. While hefting my Macintosh onto my shoulder at the airport curbside, that hated but now all-too-familiar weariness — ministry fatigue — hit my breastbone; the carrying case now felt as though it weighed fifty pounds. I dragged myself to the correct terminal, putting one step cautiously in front of the other, called home collect in order to catch David before he flew out to his scheduled meetings, then checked in at my gate. I remember breathing a quick prayer, *Lord, I think I'm going to need angels to get home.*

The only way I can describe this condition is to say it feels as though there is a chronic wound in my spirit which breaks apart and leaves me dangerously vulnerable. An exhaustion overcomes me which is more than merely physical. I hear myself saying when it comes, "Karen, you've gone *beyond* fatigue again." The weariness of my body aches in all my joints, in my jaws, behind my eyes. The weight becomes increasingly cumbersome, desperate. If I can just get home to David, to his warm and familiar physical self, to our bed, then I'll be okay.

My plane, however, was delayed in Portland due to storms over the Rockies; consequently, I missed my connecting flight from Denver to Chicago and was informed that there would be a five-hour delay before the next plane took off for O'Hare. I calculated flight times and determined I would arrive home sometime after midnight. I wondered if the limousine driver my publisher had hired would wait five hours for a customer. Probably not. What in the world could I do in this condition at O'Hare airport in order to get home? David had gone. There was no one I felt I could call in the middle of the night.

By this time I had pulled a rented cart from its rack for the Macintosh, had dragged myself to the customer service counter and was standing behind many irate passengers, all trying to get ticket changes to various destinations. Directly ahead of me in line waited a young man. When he reached the counter, I heard him state that his final destination was Chicago. As he turned from the agent, I smiled and said something simple like, "Do you suppose we'll get home to-night?" A conversation began which resulted in this young man staying with me from that moment until we disem-barked at O'Hare around 12:30, a time lapse all together of some eight hours.

He loaded his carry-on equipment onto my cart; we found a place to have dinner and used our meal vouchers provided by American Airlines to enjoy a leisurely meal; we walked back to our assigned gate and had an intriguing conversation while waiting for the last flight to O'Hare; he sat beside me after we boarded the plane; and he walked with me through the halls until we came to the security check-point where he was met by his family. My young friend was twenty-three, just graduated from college, and I was forty-three.

During that lengthy pause in his company, I discovered I was in the hands of a true gentleman, an excellent conver-sationalist, someone thoughtful and, to use an old-fashioned word, genteel. Our dinner table conversation, the get-acquainted kind, was relaxed as we discovered many common threads. I consider myself well-read in certain fields; but my companion, with twenty years less time for study, was unusually versed in literature, theology, and the relationship of one to another. We talked about Milton; we talked about Tolkien and Charles Williams and C. S. Lewis; we examined Russian writers—Dostoesvsky, Tolstoy, and Solzhenitsyn. We compared likes and dislikes, touched on the Greek dramatists, recounted which Shakespeare plays we had seen and which of modern theatre.

I could still feel the weakness within, this mysterious depletion of my strength, but I knew that for the moment I had found safe harbor. Peace surrounded me.

Some oil rig workers, a loud and noisy bunch of men, had been stranded also and were lounging in the halls of our terminal. One of them ambled into our safe circle of two, "Isn't this the pits?" he asked, coughing through the words. "A three-hour layover in Denver." He looked at me, looked at the young man beside me, and then looked back at me once more. "Hey! Why don't you come on over and join me and the guys for drinks."

I demurred, explaining that my new friend and I were having a lovely conversation; but if he were interested in the American transcendentalists, we would love to have *him* join *us* in our discussion. This was mean of me, but I was in this safe place and needed to fend off anything that would disturb or jar me. He harumphed a little, then hastened back to his drinking buddies.

I do not know who my young friend was. I cannot remember his name. I know we exchanged names. Although he played the role of guardian angel, he was certainly human: he had a girlfriend, a fianceé. I met both his father and sweetheart at O'Hare airport where they eagerly swept him out to the waiting car. "How will you get home?" he asked over his shoulder, as they hurried him toward the exit. By that time I was quite sure I would find a way.

At the baggage claim to collect my suitcases, as I waited by the rotating belt, another man approached me. "Mrs. Mains?" he asked. Surprised, I replied that I was she. He then explained that he was my limousine driver, that he'd checked on my flight time, and thought he'd better wait for me since O'Hare practically closes down after midnight. Wasn't I tired? Could he help me with my luggage and my computer? This man, who was a complete stranger to me, had waited for me for five hours (taking whatever deliveries he could in between my original arrival time and when I actually landed). He transported me gently to my front door by 2:00 A.M., Chicago time. I had stepped off the speaking platform in Cannon Beach at 11:30 A.M. (9:30 A.M. Central Standard Time) on the first leg of my trip. It had been a long day and a long journey.

The house emptied that Monday morning as teens went off to school. All was quiet; and I kept thinking, *If I just sleep and rest, I'll be better.* By noon, I was not better; the fatigue, despite sleep, seemed heavier and this quality about myself that I can only describe as vagueness — I feel as though my mind, body, and spirit are becoming *vague* — seemed to be increasing.

I telephoned my spiritual mentor who was living in Milwaukee and asked her to pray. She is a ministering person and understands these moments of spiritual exhaustion. After praying for me over the phone, she emphasized again (as I have heard from her before) that what I needed were the sacraments and that I should hie myself to my rector (or if I was too weak, call him to hie himself to me) in order to receive the anointing oil, the laying on of hands, and the elements of communion.

How in the world would I explain this to the pastor of the church where I had just begun to worship? I couldn't possibly call; but my mentor, a woman not given to hesitations, did herself.

Within an hour my rector was at my door, with the small leather case containing the silver cylinders for oil and communion in hand; and with his own family's dinner commandeered from his wife's kitchen for my boys and me.

Embarrassed by my need, I knelt (shakily) and received the fragrant oil upon my forehead, the touch of kindly hands. I was a woman in serious need of spiritual ministrations, a woman weak and fragile. That reality I had to accept. Believe me I was humbled that I would need help, humbled that anyone would take the time to care for me. And so with these things, with the touch of his fingertips marking a cross of oil upon my forehead, with gentle hands crowning my head in prayer, with the lightweight circle of the host melting on my tongue, with all this physicality, the spiritual seeping in my soul was *stanched*. It is a mystery, is it not?

In that week's mail I received a letter from the young woman at the Cannon Beach Conference Center who had led the music and worship. We had become warm friends in those few days. The gist of her message was as follows:

"I hate to write you in case I have misunderstood, but during the night of the day you left to fly home, the Lord woke me from my sleep with pressing urgency. Pray for Karen! I seemed to hear. Pray! Pray! Pray! So I did, I prayed for you off and on all night. I just need to know that you are all right. Are you well? Is your family well? Love, Judy Nelson."

So this I know. I am not alone. I do not minister alone; I am not by myself when in danger. I walk in an unseen community of care. It is all about me—above, beneath, behind, before. This is a mysterious communion, is it not, this one to which I am privy? "If one member suffers, all suffer together. . . ." There are angels on the way home.

11

The Quiltmakers

For over a year, I kept a vow of a weekly prayer time, an hour and a half long, in the chapel of St. Mark's parish church, Geneva, Illinois. Faithfully, I kept it, sweating through sweltering summers and shivering through unheated winters. Since I prayed in the afternoon, I loved in every season to watch the light through the stained-glass windows cast its colors, like tumbled jewels, onto the old wooden pews and over the worn patterned carpet above which I knelt. Here, above my head, hung the ambry light, and I noted with the passing minutes how its rose reflection climbed the brass cross above the altar.

All was quiet at St. Mark's parish church, except for the scrambling of the squirrels chasing across the peaked roof, the sound of the staff's footsteps on the stairs, or the doors of the nave opening behind me as an occasional visitor came to tour the historic chapel. Mostly, I was alone. My business followed the instructions of the traditional invitation to prayer: "Let us pray for the Church" (this I do ably) "and for the whole world" (this less so).

Over and over, and only in that place, kneeling between the gap in the gate of the communion railing which divides the nave from the sanctuary, before the altar, above the threadbare carpeting, one Scripture came to mind: the verse from Proverbs 3:6 (KJV). "In all thy ways acknowledge him, and he will direct thy paths." It was spoken to my heart personally, "In all your ways acknowledge *me*, and *I* shall direct *your* paths."

This is the second verse of two from that passage in Proverbs 3 which I memorized when I was a girl in the First Baptist Church of Wheaton, Illinois, the church where my father was the music director. The first verse, verse 5, says, "Trust in the Lord with all thine heart; and lean not unto thine own understanding." Then verse 6; "In all thy ways acknowledge him, and he shall direct thy paths."

My responsibility as a member of the church vestry was to chair the Spiritual Life Commission, which meant that the annual women's fall retreat fell to my initiative. For this year I chose making quilts as the emblem of our theme: the need for us to be stitched together in love.

First, one must choose the pattern and colors.
Then, the fabric must be cut and the piecing begins.
Next, a quilt must be put together;
The batting and backing and fronting are basted.
Lastly, the quilting takes place, the finishing it off;
And finally, one uses, enjoys, remembers,
Then hands a quilt down.

I started my planning with high ideals — we would involve as many people as possible. We should do readings, I thought, from the play *The Quilters*, which is about pioneer women and the meaning of quilts in their lives.

In the summers, we'd put up the frame on the screened porch and when the work was done for the day, Mama would say, "OK girls, let's go to it." That was the signal for good times and laughin'. We'd pull up our chairs around the frame and anyone that dropped in would do the same, even if they couldn't stitch straight. Course we'd take out their stitches later if they was really bad. But it was for talking and visiting that we put up quilts in the summer. People would get out after the chores in the summertime and oh how the word would fly that we had the frame up.

For the retreat, we would collect old, half-finished, or new quilts and mount a quilt exhibit in the narthex. We would find women who could play dulcimers and fiddles; we would serve apple fritters and mulled cider, and order box lunches to be carried to nearby homes—Martha's Circle, Vivienne's Circle, Alice's Circle—for the Saturday noon meal. Certainly the largest number of women would want to attend this retreat. And the committee . . . ah, the committee! We would pray together, we would work together, we would become stitched together in love. (My nature is prone to these idealized prognostications. My mother was a poet and a romantic. The tendency is in my blood, and it has caused me endless grief.)

Well, I had not anticipated a fall flu epidemic and the effect of my heavy travel schedule, which kept pulling me away from my plans. Nor did I know that the weekend I had chosen would be chock-full of professional conferences, spiritual seminars, school events, etc. And the committee . . . ah, the committee; the first time we met as a full committee, without one of the members sick in bed with aches and pains, was the week before the retreat.

Each woman in the committee worked hard at her appointed task, but I seemed to be blocked in many of my efforts. I wrote out assignments for volunteers—several significant jobs were not taken, people said no, the announcement didn't make the church newsletter. Needless to say, several weeks before our retreat date, I began to experience major frustration. The publicity was not building in a way that would net a good attendance.

Postcards with the picture of a quilt and Luci Shaw's poem were mailed as invitations to each church woman:

> To keep a husband and five children warm,
>   she stitched quilts thick as drifts against
> the door. Through every fleshy square, white threads
>   needled their almost invisible tracks; her hours
>   walked each small stitch that held together
>   the raw-cut, uncolored edges of her life.
>
> She pieced them beautiful, and summer-bright,
>   to thaw her frozen soul. Under her fingers
>   the scraps grew to green birds, and purple,
> improbable leaves; deeper than calico, her mid-winter
>   mind burst into flowers. She watched them bloom
>   between the double stars, the wedding rings. [1]

Luci's poem could not have conveyed a more appealing invitation, and yet the conference refused to come together. I have enough spiritual experience to know that blocked doors can mean that something is not right with me. One afternoon, praying quietly in the church sanctuary, I asked, "What are You trying to teach me, Lord?"

The next day, Edith Gibson called. This is a woman of grace and style, in her late middle years, who teaches etiquette classes to children and is an instructor in dance. I had asked her to see if she remembered a child's game we could use with the women after the lunch break. "I do remember one," Edith said. "I think it fits your quilt theme. It's a line game we used to play when we were girls." Then she sang:

> The thread follows the needle,
> the thread follows the needle.
> In and out the needle goes
> While mother sews the children's
>   clothes.

---

1. "Quiltmakers" reprinted from *Polishing the Petoskey Stone*, copyright 1990 by Luci Shaw. Used by permission of Harold Shaw Publishers, Wheaton, IL.

Perfect! I remembered this playground game myself. The girl at the end of the line (the needle) leads the rest (the thread) in and out through the uplifted arms of the girls at the near end of the line, with each one turning as they pass through. Then suddenly I realized: that was what the Lord was trying to say to me. *The thread follows the needle; the thread follows the needle.* "In all your ways acknowledge me, and I will direct your paths." In a sense the Holy Spirit was whispering, *Karen Mains, get your controlling hands off this retreat. This is my retreat. I will be the Quiltmaker who stitches together the pieces of this church quilt. We will piece this together. You and I. But I will plan the pattern. The needle is in my hand and you are the thread.* And so in the busy last days of preparing the retreat, I remembered Edith's low voice singing over the telephone: *The thread follows the needle; the thread follows the needle.*

What wonderful freedom! I began to sit back and watch this Master Quilter piece together the quilt that was our church women's retreat. "Oh, I have an unfinished quilt on a frame. Shall I bring that?" someone asked. By all means. "Linda has lovely handmade baskets. Shall we have her bring them for the exhibit?" By all means. "I think we should have retreat evaluation sheets. I've already typed them into my computer. Is that all right?" The woman who had taken over the responsibilities for the Friday evening Reader's Theatre designed the printed program for the play—no work for me.

The thread follows the needle, the thread follows the needle—I continually took my hands off and let myself be a thread run through the eye of the needle.

Before the retreat itself, everyone brought quilts in various stages of completion—like our own lives. I will admit that my heart paused when the night came to mount all the quilts for the exhibit. We had collected a huge pile of assorted quilts. How were we going to get them all displayed? Again, the whisper to my heart, *See, I am the Quiltmaker, I am patching the pieces. I am putting the Quilt all together. Wait until you see the beautiful finished design.*

The curate's wife and one of my committee members (the other two had been instructed to stay home to recover fully from the flu) pitched in and within a couple of hours we had established a beautiful ordered arrangement from chaos; log cabin designs, four doves in a window, the lone star, crosses and losses, windmill, the rebel patch, baby's block, robbing Peter to pay Paul, double wedding rings. We filled antique tables and chairs and hung quilts on the walls; we spread the most beautiful patterns over the backs of the church pews.

At the retreat the quilts shone in the dim lights as the readers read the words of women's thoughts from American times past and we sang old hymns to the accompaniment of an autoharp.

Enough women attended to make our efforts worthwhile. All the committee members recovered from the flu in time to attend the retreat. And I was very aware I couldn't have done it on my own. When the thread follows the needle in God's hand, we often learn that He is calling us to undertake the big tasks by working together on the quilter's frame.

Some gifts that people give to us they never know they have given. Now, whenever I rush ahead in my planning, whenever I fill my life with more events than one woman can possibly accomplish, I hear Edith Gibson's voice singing a chant song. *The thread follows the needle, the thread follows the needle, in and out the needle goes.*

And I see the women of St. Mark's parish bending in line, hands joined. I remember the laughing women, young and old, some pregnant, some single, some married, passing in and out of each other's arms, performing the movements of a children's playground game.

I have come to understand that I am being stitched into this patchwork. I am a part of the design of our common life. In this church I can be me, Karen Mains, a member of the laity, a committee woman doing corporate tasks. Here, I plan the retreat, do the work; and someone else, another speaker, receives the acclaim.

At the Wednesday morning Eucharist, during the passing of the peace, one man whose daughter died in her twenties and I make a big deal about embracing. For that moment, he is my father and I am his child. Another man in his seventies, the former chairman of Quaker Oats, and I pass the peace by making a sign from the language of the deaf. Each of us touches a forefinger to our thumb, which we link like the magician links his steel hoops—mine to his, his to mine. The sign means "to be joined." As a patch in this common quilt which God is stitching together, I have a place here. I am "joined." I feel like I can kick off my shoes if I want. I have an invitation to every church supper. And I am wanted. *The thread follows the needle.*

12

Prison Mates

On January 10, 1983, I visited the Israeli Defense Force headquarters in the war-devastated city of Sidon, Lebanon. My
party and I were to be briefed on the June 1982 Israeli invasion
of Lebanon and the rationale for its continuing military occupation. Outside the gates stood a group of Arab women,
their heads kerchiefed, their skirts brushing their ankles.
Dark eyes stared, piercing. A few questions in Arabic were
asked, questions I could not understand. Mostly the women
were silent, watching, watching. Some stood, some squatted.
Their eyes burned our backs as the gates closed behind us
and we walked into the shadows of the armed forces' concrete compound.

"Who are those women?" I asked. I was told that they
were Palestinian and Lebanese wives whose husbands had
been taken captive. The women came every day for months
and did not know the whereabouts of their sons and husbands. Throughout the military briefing, my mind kept
wandering to the vigil of the women outside the gates.
Where were their husbands? How old were their sons? Were
they alive or dead? Had they been tortured? Were they

hungry, cold, or ill? Was there no one to take pity and allevi-
ate their anxieties? (But then, that is what war is all about, is
it not?—callous disregard for other men, for their wives, for
their mothers, for their sweethearts.)

Research informed me that after the Israeli invasion in June
1981, the Israeli Defense Force arrested all adult male
Palestinians, as well as any Lebanese or foreigners who had
supposed connections with the Palestinian Liberation
Organization. According to the *Washington Post* of July 23,
1982, "The Israeli blitz has changed the face of the region.
There appear to be virtually no Palestinian men between the
ages of 16 and 60 free in southern Lebanon."

After indiscriminate arrests, most prisoners spent a few
days in interrogation centers and were finally bussed to the
al-Ansar prison camp near Nabatiyyah. The prison at
al-Ansar, where most were eventually detained, was built in
ten days by Israeli contractors. A large compound confined
by a high dirt embankment topped with barbed wire, its
housing consisted of tents pitched in rows of 300 each on
packed sand. The 212 boys under the age of sixteen who
were allowed to leave reported "sardine-like" overcrowding;
a requirement that all detainees remain stretched out on a
blanket at all times; beatings, starvation, and some deaths;
and the presence of only one doctor for the prisoners and no
infirmary (*Washington Post*, July 28, 1982). The Israelis, on
the other hand, claimed that the prisoners enjoyed freedom
of movement and a clinic in each compound (*Christian Sci-
ence Monitor*, August 5, 1982). No journalists, however, had
been allowed open access to the prison camp.

Through the years I have remembered the Arab women.
Their vigil symbolizes my deepest fears as a woman: that I
will some day be prevented from easing the pain of those I
love; a son unjustly detained, a husband tortured for his faith,
a daughter starving in solitary confinement. Even living in
a free nation, I, too, have kept my share of vigils. This is
women's work, to watch the approach of the inexorable and
to suffer—in death wards, by hospital beds, in trauma units,

in nursing homes—waiting for bad news, waiting for the worst that can happen.

The Arab women's vigil came rushing at me again out of memory when David and I received a letter from Argentina. We learned later that it had been smuggled out of a jail in Mexico City. The letter was dated, "Day #8, Wed, March 11/87," and it came from Ed Aulie, a missionary to Mexico. The letter read:

> I was arrested a week ago and taken to Mexico City on an all night bus ride. Since then I've been in jail, charged with falsified documents, 6–12 months in prison—I was shocked.... Now that I have a couple of lawyers on this, the problem is not my documents at all but the Governor's office in Tabasco wants me out. My lawyers tell me it's strictly a political case, a smear job....
>
> My greatest fear in life has been to be in a Mexican prison and beaten or pawed by a pervert. Humanly speaking those fears are well founded, but every day I awaken with joy to be alive and to be here with these inmates, the most helpless, powerless, destitute, and forgotten lot I have ever known. Each day I weep with different men and boys. Their stories of tragedy rip me up. We are let out of our cells at 9:30 A.M. to walk in a cement courtyard smaller than a basketball court. At 10 we are given a scoop of rice and beans that would not fill my baby boy Erik. At 6:30 another cup of water or coffee and at 7 we are locked up for the night. I ache to be with Denise and the children, but I know God has me here for a high purpose. The hours fly by each day. A day is not long enough. Most of these men are soon open to Christ. They devour every word and have a hundred questions and a thousand regrets. Four Nicaraguans have made faith commitments, a man from Peru, 3 from Belize, a U.S. businessman is under conviction and a man from Belgium is still arguing. . . .

Ed, the son of missionary parents, had been in our high school group at Moody Memorial Church in Chicago, during which time David led him to the Lord. As a young man, while working through a personal trauma he had come to live for a year and a half in our pastorate home, helping me considerably in the task of raising my kids while David was occupied with the demands of an inner-city pastorate. When Ed married Denise, we even went on the couple's honeymoon. (We gave them a trip to the Shakespeare Festival in Ontario, with the proviso that we be allowed to provide transportation!) My spiritual son, a brother who had been part of our family, this close, close friend, was in prison. David and I went to our knees in prayer.

But I could not get my faint prayers past the guards or the chain-link fences with their razor-wire tops. And no one could give me information about the well-being of the one inside. I grieved as though for my own child. I labored in worry. My prayers were waylaid by a concrete fasthold as real as that IDF cement compound in Sidon. My education hindered me as well; I have studied the prison literature of the world and know the character types who populate these hellholes. Lives eke away day by day, year by year, decade by decade. I was an Arab woman keeping vigil outside closed prison doors.

One night I lay in bed, tossing, my prayers dropping on the carpet beside me. Rereading the smuggled letter, I thought about prayers of praise. God was working through Ed among those prisoners, he was bringing the light of Christ into their cells. Did I truly believe what I preached? Prison walls and evil bureaucracy could close in this one we loved, but they could not close out our God. Copying Paul and Silas of old, I intentionally rejoiced over the fact that a sovereign God can use unregenerate men's designs for his own purposes. Anxiety released its clutch in the face of praise, and love came rushing in, turning my prayers deeply empathic, not only for Ed but for Christians imprisoned all over the world.

The words from Hebrews 13 came pushing at me, "Remember those who are in prison, as though in prison with them" (v. 3, RSV). So I did. Suddenly! Suddenly! The prison gates opened and my soul shoved gladly past the barricades. Love found Ed, somewhere fastbound in a Mexican cell.

I prayed for Ed, as though with him. Finally, through prayer, I touched his face with tenderness; I lifted the tin cup of cold, clean water for him to drink; I held my body close to his to make him warm; I chafed his hands with my own, blowing on them and rubbing them briskly. I lifted a bowl of pungent broth, healthy and nourishing to his lips; I broke bread, black and thick, from the loaf for him. Then the light came, angels shimmering in the darkness. Holding each other, we two humans lifted our heads to laugh the old joke of the centuries, a secret riddle known to imprisoned Christians. Christ is near in solitary confinements.

Two days later, we received word that Ed had been released from prison. Now lest anyone overvalue my prayers, calculations comparing dates and times and mail deliveries revealed that Ed had actually been released before my midnight vigil. This was not particularly troublesome to me, because I learned a powerful truth. There are prayers which go where the body cannot follow, and we cannot dream the work of God they do.

Irina Ratushinskaya, the Christian poet and author of the book *Pencil Letters*, tells about being in the icy-cold prison of a Soviet punishment block and yet feeling warmth: "Believe me, it was often thus: / In solitary cells, on winter nights / A sudden sense of joy and warmth / And then, unsleeping, I would know / A-huddle by an icy wall: / Someone is thinking of me now. . . ." [1]

Who knows, when we pray for prisoners "as though in prison with them" where our prayers go? Who knows when I labor to write to the best of my ability, when that labor becomes so intense as to be prayer, who knows how it is used? Perhaps another writer, better than I, is strengthened to write at his best level, until his work becomes art. And when love comes rushing into all of this, who knows what we do, who is warmed and where?

---

1. From *Pencil Letters* by Irina Ratushinskaya, copyright 1989. Used by permission of Alferd A. Knopf, Inc. (New York) and Andrew Nurnberg Associates, Ltd. (London).

The theologian Teilhard de Chardin has written, "The day will come when, having mastered the ether, the wind, the tides, and gravity, we will harness the energies of love for God. And then for the second time in the history of the world, we will discover fire." All my life I have been taught that prayer is powerful; but I learned while praying for Ed Aulie that prayer linked with love is unfathomably powerful. And who knows, who knows who was warmed in what prison, in what part of the world by my woman prayers?

I hope to be present for the second time in the history of the world when we discover fire.

PART IV

*Befriending
the Stranger*

13

Tin Cup and a Passerby

I had become a beggar woman banging my tin cup on the sidewalk. "A pittance! A pittance!" I cried. "A pittance for poor writers!" Editors would approach me for book possibilities, and I would suggest to them this great idea of a financial grant (from their publishers) to establish some kind of professional writers' association.

My strong suspicion was that few contemporary Christian writers were creating real art, work with classic potential, because we were so isolated from one another. This grant would fund, I explained, not the novice but a group of working writers who had proven their sincere intent and who (with evaluation, friendship, and idea-exchange) had potential to do better. As an example, I cited the "Inklings" in England. This group included the influential writers C. S. Lewis, Charles Williams, J. R. R. Tolkien, *et al.*, who did better work because of their exchange with each other.

In the remarkable book, *Creativity: The Magic Synthesis*, the author Silvano Arieti, explains which conditions in a society best enhance the fermentation process of creativity. He calls this atmosphere "the creativogenic society" and lists

nine categories, the eighth of which is "interaction of significant persons." It seemed to me that evangelical publishing, which makes money off the Christian writer, should
also invest something in the future of our artistic community.
My tin-cup pitch, my beggar-woman's claim, was that the
Christian writer could not become the best that he or she
could be without a regular "interaction of significant persons" (i.e., other writers who strive for excellence).

Everyone I talked with—and I introduced the idea to
members of all echelons of the major evangelical publishing
establishments—everyone thought this was a grand idea
(yes, a necessary idea); but no one offered a penny of financial support. My tin cup stayed empty; and for about four
years, I kept banging it on the sidewalk but no passerby
stopped to hear my cry. Still, I wailed on: "Nurture the gifts
of the artist, and the artist's gifts will nurture the community!" I wish I could say that this beggary was wholly altru-
istic. Mostly, I think my tin-cup banging was because I was
lonely as a Christian writer, lonely as a person with artistic
sensibilities in the evangelical community.

I simply could not make significant creative connections.
To begin with, I was a woman attempting to function artis-
tically in a broad community which mistrusted symbol, the
artist's tool. In addition, my woman's time was not my own.
I not only raised four children to comparative emotional,
psychological, and spiritual health, but during a fifteen-year
period, there were only one-and-a-half years when David
and I didn't have someone (often a fragmented young adult)
living in our home. When I was thirty-three my father began
a death march, due to encephalitis, which took four long
years to complete. A couple of years later, my mother died
on my thirty-ninth birthday; and two of our children
survived life-threatening illnesses: Melissa survived a
three-month fever of unidentified origin, and Joel was
carried to the hospital emergency room in a meningitis-
induced coma. Mounds of laundry and malfunctioning

sump pumps thumped out their demands for my energy. Life with children was often a pet parade of unimaginable proportions, from the fish in the four aquariums to the pinto horse stabled in the high school Spanish teacher's shed, from the flea-carrying Old English sheepdog to the proliferating bunnies in the rabbit hutch.

I somehow learned to be a broadcaster; took up—reluctantly—an itinerant traveling ministry; made it to school plays; hosted yearly homecoming float-making in our garage; fed the high school soccer team chili after games waged on sodden fall playing fields; toted kids to college in a station wagon loaded with cast-off furniture to set up dorm rooms, college houses, and apartments; and made pals out of my teens' rejected dates. There simply hadn't been time, as yet, to form or join a "creativogenic society" (if I could have found one, that is).

In addition, the inexorable ticking of my mortal clock marched on. A xeroxed page, taped to the inside of one of my kitchen cupboards, is titled "Very Good News for Your 40th Birthday"; and it contains a list of achievers whose work did not reach its apex until after that landmark nativity date. Raymond Chandler published his first novel, *The Big Sleep*, at 51. Julia Child took the mystery out of French cooking when *The French Chef* aired on WGBH–TV. She was 50. John Milton was 59 when he published *Paradise Lost*. Dwight Eisenhower won recognition as a military commander at 52 and was elected to the presidency at 62. George Eliot published her first full-length novel, *Adam Bede*, when she was 40. Joseph Conrad published *Heart of Darkness* when he was 45.

This list I reiterate to myself with each passing birthdate. It is of some comfort. An advancing time-line is not necessarily a disadvantage, but what was I to do about this aching loneliness in regard to my own writer's reality? Who was I as a writer? What were my potentialities? What were my limits? Which mistakes was I, in ignorance, making? What in my education did I need to supplement? What were the current thoughts that would stimulate my own thinking? Most importantly, how could I integrate my faith into creative work without damaging the artistic content?

Well, need can make one bold. A hungry soul cannot starve for long without crying out "Bread! Bread!" (or stealing it). At a convention for National Religious Broadcasters, I had a first-time meeting with a publisher, Kip Jordon from Word Publishing. Bang-bang-bang. My tin cup hit the Sheraton coffee-shop tabletop. Bang-bang-bang. I went through my beggar's lament. Without my expecting it, the feet of this passerby stopped; my cry for pittance was heard. I found my mug stuffed with the promise of a generous grant—no strings attached.

With this largess and in collusion with Richard Foster, writer and religion professor at Friends University, Wichita, Kansas, as well as with the aid of Calvin Miller, prolific writer and Southern Baptist pastor in Lincoln, Nebraska, the Chrysostom Society was launched. There are twenty-two writers (or twenty-three, depending on how you count!) and an assortment of spouses. We meet officially once a year and encourage cross-pollination between yearly convocations.

Why recount this story, this crossing between one lonely writer and a publisher with a heart beyond his own narrow publishing confines and a resulting collaboration of writers? Most of my readers are not writers, and you may be wondering why you should care about this. Because, I would say, this story addresses the alienation so many of us feel in our work these days, no matter our fields of endeavor. In *Working*, Studs Terkel chronicles the despair of the average working person. "This book, being about work, is, by its very nature, about violence—to the spirit as well as to the body. . . . It is, above all, about daily humiliations. . . . It is about a search, too, for daily meaning . . . for a sort of life rather than for a Monday through Friday sort of dying. . . ."

Most of my readers are not writers, but many of my readers are lonely—lonely in their work, lonely in their daily lives, lonely in their homes, lonely in their churchlife. Carl Sandburg once wrote, "Give me hunger. . . . Give me your shabbiest, weariest hunger! . . . But leave me a little love . . . A voice to speak to me in the day end . . . A hand to touch me in the dark room. . . ." Most of us, no matter our occupation, need others. We need a society, an understanding community, a group of peers; a voice to speak to us at day's end, a hand to touch in the dark.

One of the greatest tools worked by our Dark Enemy, the father of alienations, is to keep humans separate. We must labor to say "No!" to his intent. We must struggle as a people of faith to form into communities with common commitments; we must insist on covenantal relationships; we must model to our lonely world the endless variety of ways in which we, the church, can make significant human connections.

God is often a divine prankster. He expects us to look back and laugh at the Punch-and-Judy tragicomedy of our own lives. Because I have tasted creative loneliness, I've started an Artist's Colony in my local church. I sit in the writers' workshop, or the visual artists' sharing sessions, deeply moved by the affirmation I see, by the encouragement, by the resulting growth in artistic expression. I am also starting a Christian Writer's Cabal for my own geographic territory, intended for fiction writers who wish to go about the enterprise of helping one another create better fiction. The laugh is on me! I didn't need a national writer's gathering. A creativogenic society is nearby. But our national group serves as a contemporary model for many other regional groups; my loneliness was used to stimulate the formulation of a part for the sake of the whole.

I know I have been made strong for this local organization because I have a place, a once-a-year fellowship of former strangers, this valuable list of phone numbers I can call, these members of Chrysostom's. A voice at the day's end, a touch in the dark. Being a part of a collegial association has given me strength enough to find my own way in the rest of my professional life. I am aware I have a debt to pay, and I am paying it.

Every day of the week, I set aside one hour for the work of intercessory prayer. The time on Thursdays is given to prayers for Christian writers and artists; for those of the Chrysostom Society—Harold, Richard, Emilie and William, Alice and Steve, John, Madeleine, Calvin, Andrea and Keith, Rudy and Shirley, Virginia, Eugene, Luci, Robert, Walter, Larry, Gregory, and Philip. And I also pray for those artists in the world whom God is drawing to Himself, that they will find him. I pray that we will do good work, that others will have "interaction with significant persons," that one favor, given generously, from people we scarcely know, for the sake of a broader cause, can have untold benefits for God's grand design.

14

The Surrogate Mother

Genealogies can be intriguing if one takes the time to pursue their complexities. A phrase from Exodus 6:20 raises all kinds of questions. "Amran took to wife Jochebed his father's sister and she bore him Aaron and Moses . . . " (RSV). Did Amran really marry his own aunt? Was his wife his own grandfather's child? Or were the two simply cousins as some scholars suggest? Moreover, what kind of woman was this Jochebed, named only in the genealogies, who gave birth to two such outstanding children that they became the leaders of the Israeli exodus?

I had cause to think about Jochebed one May morning as I sat in a vestibule of a building in New Harmony, Indiana, listening to trained actors practice a script on which I had collaborated. I began to appreciate the defiance of such a woman who, despite the edict of the Egyptian king, would not put her own infant son to death ("when she saw that he was a goodly child, she hid him three months . . ."). I was thinking about Moses' mother because, in a sense, I had surrendered a much-loved child into the hands of a surrogate mother.

This tale begins with a phone call from a new acquaintance. Gwen Mansfield wanted to put my book, *The Fragile Curtain*, into feature-length script form. I laughed and said, "But you'll only have a documentary. There's no story line. The book is about my journey through many of the refugee camps of the world." Still we decided, at her urging, to collaborate on a script since there were several themes from the journey that I had been thinking about working into fiction, one of which was the deep meaning of the meeting of strangers. We made arrangements for working sessions with the goal of establishing the narrative line within portions of my refugee book.

Gwen was one of those strangers I had met at another writers' conference where we both were on the teaching staff. After becoming a Christian, she and her husband had conducted a drama ministry called Royal Diadem, and she had written scripts for several Christian films. I learned that Gwen was determined to turn her acting and stage experience into a scriptwriting career. Gwen felt called to mount an undaunted assault upon that impregnable fortress, the secular media industry.

So we met. Mooching off my friends on the West Coast, we holed up in Long Beach; in Bellingham, Washington; and in Redding, California. At each of these sessions we worked for several days straight, taking breaks only for walks, a movie (to stimulate our scriptwriting sensibilities), or a meal. The evenings were given to long talks. A successful collaboration is as much a matter of good relationship as it is of ability. Seeing that one of us was from Poulsbo, Washington, and the other from just outside Chicago, these getting-to-know-you sessions were important — the distance between us might cause future misunderstandings if we did not draw close now. I discovered that Gwen was deadly serious about our work whereas the project was more an exercise in creativity for me, a lark — at least at the beginning.

A collaboration is also a matter of each contributor understanding clear professional lines. I have friends for whom co-authoring projects have turned into nightmares. Sometimes ownership, responsibility, and the subsequent disbursement of fees become issues. So, as much as possible, we made sure that what could be made clear was made clear. Gwen and I decided that if anything would come of our collaboration, the credit lines would read:

Script by Gwen Mansfield.
Story by Gwen Mansfield and Karen Burton Mains.

In effect, this meant that Gwen held final editorial say; that she would do the bulk of the work; that she would be responsible for the marketing of the final product; that if it were optioned, she would hire a lawyer; and that if the sky should fall and *Common Ground* (as she titled it) were awarded the Oscar for best screenplay, she would attend the ceremony and receive the prize. I agreed to a small percentage of the financial point system (the means by which the film industry metes out its royalties), a credit line (if the vagaries of the Hollywood industry didn't so damage the story intent that I couldn't allow my name to be included in the credits), and perhaps a boost for my book now out of print.

This all seemed exceedingly fair. There would be no script without Gwen's dream. Apart from the initial concept, my time would require about nine days of collaboration, several phone consultations, and some later script readings; but Gwen's labor would be months' worth of effort without any financial guarantees or subsidies.

I had never entertained serious ambitions regarding scriptwriting. I want to form the fiction, the short stories, the chancel drama from which filmscripts are made. So I would give credit to Gwen.

As she drew me into the project, I became entranced with the creative exercises. Talking out dialogue together was stimulating! Setting scenes, calling characters to life, challenged me. But that anything would come of this effort still seemed to me a pipedream.

Months after our last work session I received a long-distance phone call from Gwen saying that the script had won a place in The New Harmony Project. This is an unusual opportunity in which writers' works undergo evaluation by professionals in the field who commit themselves to helping the writer improve his ability through mounting the piece as a workshop exercise. Three plays and three filmscripts are accepted each year. The winning writers gather in New Harmony, Indiana (a historic, restored community, far from the beaten track, but ideal for creative work), where the board gives initial manuscript evaluations.

The Project is a two-part process: first, an initial review, after which the writers are sent home to rewrite the works; then a two-week laboratory in which directors, stage and screen actors, television writers, sound and film crews all converge and the rewritten scripts are reworked again! Portions of the play are mounted. Scenes from the script are shot, and after much arduous effort, final read-throughs are provided by the professional actors.

I was thrilled for Gwen, applauded her tenacity, and had to admit to being surprised. Particularly was I surprised when I found myself driving down to New Harmony, Indiana, wedging a short visit in between my husband's leave-taking for ten days in India and a weekend board meeting of a national campus organization of which I am a trustee. My collaborator had called and said, "Karen, is there any way you can come down? A couple of the board members wondered if you were going to make it."

When I arrived, I immediately plunged into the artistic community. Breakfast-table conversations were intense discussions on the meaning of published writers and their works. Dialogues continued past midnight as we pondered the mysteries of the creative process. I will never forget sitting with my chin practically on the shoulder of the director, with Gwen, script in hand, perched in the writer's seat beside him; all of us watching the video monitor. A film crew was shooting the tent scene she had chosen, supposedly taking place in the Northern Frontier District of Pakistan, but instead, positioned here in a cornfield in Indiana! I listened to professional actors speak lines I had helped to write. The dialogue worked. The lines carried the subtext. And it all felt so good. (*How did I get here?* I wondered. And then, *Why has it taken me so long?*)

No wonder I had been lonely; I was suffering from acute homesickness. I realized I had spent all my life among a strange people, acclimating myself, speaking a second language. Now without any planning on my part, I had landed in familiar territory, among kin, folk who knew my native tongue, who all shared a primary kind of literacy. No longer did I have to struggle to make myself understood.

In some strange way evangelicalism has turned out not to be my country of spiritual origin after all. It has an inherent drive toward conformity; I, toward divergency. An advisor said to me recently, "Karen, you don't do anything like anyone else! You don't even perform the laying-on-of-hands like anyone else." And so I have felt out of place. I try not to offend. At the same time, I try to be true to my own best instincts. But I have come to understand that I am a refugee, a displaced person in this churchdom, and the resettlement has been hard.

The morning of the final reading (after I had typed fresh copy for Gwen for nearly sixteen hours straight so that the actors would have usable scripts after all the rewrites), I sat in the vestibule and realized that I had given my child away. A sharp pain seared me. I bit my tongue, pursed my lips. I needed to remain silent, even as I longed to coo over my baby, to brush away the fallen hairlock, to touch the soft cheek. I had given the child away by my own free will, by my own choice. I was a Hebrew wife watching from the bullrushes as a surrogate mother ordered the discipline, the care and feeding, the education of my child. I understood Jochebed.

Actors' voices came to my hearing, a choir interpreting all our words — Gwen's, mine, theirs (screen work is truly a collaborative effort); but beneath it all I heard another voice speaking, ". . . and she put the child at the river's edge among the reeds." Then the question, *And do you believe enough in my creative work going out into the world that you will give away any of your artistic children if I ask it of you? Do you?*

And I said yes, knowing this Questioner enough to know he is capable of requiring this sacrifice. I kept saying yes as I drove the seven and a half hours back to Chicago. And it hurt. It hurt all the way. But the next morning, mucking around in my perennial garden, mud impacted around the soles of my garden boots, earth beneath my fingernails, a baby was given back to me, an infant to suckle at my breast. A novel — full and rich, with what one literary critic has called the "triune intuition of creation, fall, and redemption" — began to be born in me. Central to its plot was the offering of a child to a surrogate mother. One must live first, then write.

Common Ground, through intermediary contacts, found its way to the hands of a signatory agent and began making rounds. Who knows where it is now? Hollywood is a script graveyard, and I am told this story needs a star and some twenty-million dollars in order to bring it to life.

So, I gave the child away. There was no future for it without another mother, and I am completely reconciled. For after all, we have traded gifts, Gwen and I. Such is the necessary symbiotic exchange of people from my true land. From me to her, a child; from her to me, passage to my hidden home where I don't even need to dwell to feel its effect. I just need to know that it is there and that I have entered its terrain, and that one day I will go to it again. Just now I am busy wetnursing this baby.

15

The Perennial Garden

In my deepest self, I am a gardener. I am the kind of woman who responds to her husband's casual question, "How was your day?" with a rapturous "Oh, David! Today I put my own homemade compost on the rose bushes." I am never so happy as when I am planning garden plots, hoeing out weeds, pausing to watch the morning sky, listening to the outside world, or smelling the herbal scents from the kitchen bed by the back door.

For me, gardening is following one of my blisses. The mythologist Joseph Campbell, whose interviews with Bill Moyers were transcribed into the book, *The Power of Myth*, explains that "following one's bliss" means trekking upon the life paths that bring us to those places of deepest contentment. Few people, he feels, have the courage to honor this personal call to penetrate into the knowledge of their own mysterious selves.

I consider this a concept that is in many — though not all — respects compatible with a Christian understanding of vocation: when we "follow our bliss," we are being obedient to the image of God in which we are created. When I am following my bliss, I am somehow, paradoxically, most unconscious of myself; a happy self-forgetfulness overcomes me, a child-like innocence which leaves me susceptible to stabs of the divine — these are indicators that I'm pointed in the right direction. There are moments while writing when I can't distinguish between work and worship. I'm often ecstatic when I'm absorbed by a complex learning project. I have an insatiable curiosity about other humans and become wonderfully at peace in getting to know them better. I am particularly joyful when I am gardening, when my hands are full of dirt, when I bring them to my face to smell the earth, in a form of unconscious prayer.

In *For the Life of the World*, the Russian Orthodox priest Alexander Schmemann expresses what I feel when I garden:

> The first, the basic definition of man, is that he is the priest. He stands in the center of the world and unifies it in his act of blessing God, of both receiving the world from God and offering it to God — and by filling the world with this eucharist [thanksgiving], he transforms his life, the one that he receives from the world, into life in God, into communion with Him. The world was created as the "matter," the material of one all-embracing eucharist, and man was created as the priest of this cosmic sacrament.

So, I am priestess of this small plot of grass and woods and garden. This is why I cannot resist touching the granite stone, warmed by sun and sparkling with light; why I gather crackling pods to bring home for arrangements upon the mantel and dinner table — why I must brush my hands against the flaming leaves of the burning bush. I am blessing these things, offering them back to the Creator. The cuttings of experience transplanted into my rocky soil receive my planting prayer. *Grow small thing. Grow to the glory of the Lord. Lift your flowering heads to the sun and praise God with leaf and stem. Extol your Creator by being what He has created you to be.*

I've also thought much of the deprivation caused by being denied our bliss. We have lived in our present home for some thirteen years. I was amazed to discover, my first gardening year, that the Illinois soil in our yard was clay — sticky, unyielding, and given to clotting when it rained. When I first turned the soil around our house with a spade, I found nary an earthworm. Very bad news, as any gardener knows. It's taken me ten years to create good topsoil. I've turned green matter into the ground and burned endless leaves in order to mix the ash into this clay. I've rototilled the ground, mixing in bags of pulverized dirt, and buried biodegradable garbage as my father taught me to do years ago. Worms slither everywhere through the topsoil now.

My gardening has to compete with travel schedules, with writing and broadcasting deadlines, with the demands of mothering and ministry. Our yard is full of shade, and I study the sun-fall assiduously to determine which spots receive the six hours of light per day requisite for green growth. In addition, this calling seems to be a solo calling in my family of six. No one else — neither husband nor offspring — has indicated any of the bliss which commands my soul at the first whiff of damp spring. I'm on my own in this gardening enterprise, and I will confess to discouragement, peevishness, and failure — all resulting from my own neglect. Many is the time I've just given up and let the garden go to weed. I've resigned myself to loss, rationalizing that I have more important things to do; but the emotional loss has been a wound that would not heal.

This year, however, has been different. I've had a gardening friend. This new friend, Pat, has encouraged me to pursue my own bliss. She came last fall and we marked off the area of the yard where the most sun fell. This was the narrow strip of land between the front of the house and the road, a region rife with bramble, wild blackberries, and native honeysuckle. Once the thornbushes had been torn out, the weeds mowed, and the ground turned, I discovered fairly decent black soil—a surprise! I had become resigned to a sea of clay.

I wondered if Pat would return in the spring, as she had promised. I have become very cautious about vaulting hopes, about people who make casual promises. But there she was again, early in the season; this time with a garden design in hand. We spaced out places for imaginary plants and staked the spots with green bamboo sticks, each one marked by yellow tags bearing the proper plant names. "Your husband's going to think we're growing sticks with yellow flags," Pat said, stepping off growing spaces between these markers.

I laughed with more energy than Pat might have anticipated, because my gardening efforts have become a family joke. My loved ones might, indeed, consider stakes and flags a new scheme that could only fail like all the others.

My friend Pat came Monday after Monday after Monday, her station wagon loaded with divisions from her own garden. Together we dug and transplanted and watered. We planted columbine, delphinium, astilbe; we transplanted Siberian iris, bachelor's-buttons, goose's neck. And in between the perennials, for quick encouragement, we placed forget-me-nots and Johnny-jump-ups. "Do you know," said my new friend as she hauled cardboard boxes full of green cuttings from her wagon, "I think I've started as many as fifteen-or-so gardens. I always bring transplants like this from my own yard. The more I give away, the more it seems I have to give away."

I saw my friend's mature garden in full bloom early this summer. I'd gone to shovel manure from her pile into empty garbage cans stashed in the back of my station wagon. Pat's garden was glorious, blooming in full splendor to the praise of the Creator. I suspect that one of the reasons my friend's garden does so bloomingly well is that Pat selflessly, joyfully, and eagerly shares all she has with those ready to receive it. She truly has the ministry of gardening.

Gardening is a parable of following one's bliss. Each plant grows best in the particular environment for which it was designed. Shade-loving plants grow best in shade; sun-loving plants thrive in the light. Some plants prefer alkaline soil; others take to acidity. But each plant expresses its own particular nature. A rose is a rose is a rose. It is not a daisy. So it is with the people of God's kingdom. We each grow best in the environment for which God created us; when we find that place, we are content (blissful) to be who he created us to be. I am trying to find my native soil, the right pH balance, the right nutrients, so that my roots can spread themselves, cling, and finally, reach deep.

David came home from work and found me muddy, sweaty, dirt-stained. "Ah," he said, noting my obvious bliss despite my dishevelment. "I can see you have had a Karen Mains' kind of day." Yes, utterly forgetful of self, I had been standing in the center of my world, offering it back as a blessing to God, and in the joyful labor of that eucharistic action, I was being transformed.

I have learned another spiritual principle from the gift of my gardening friend, Pat. Gardening, like the work of Christ's people, is best accomplished in community, not in isolation. That's where the ideal of "following your bliss" shows its flaws. We are not autonomous selves with a destiny apart from all others; we can only be who we were intended to be in relation to others, which is, I think, a reflection of our God, who is, in himself, a "community" of three persons.

Apart from others, the perversity of the world steals into our most treasured activities. We need support even in the worthwhile things we, for the most part, enjoy. I might be tempted to let the weeding go because of a too-full calendar, but I know that Pat will be checking on things Monday, so I make an effort to keep the tedious labor on schedule. I have weed seeds in this new plot. It will be several years before the weeding becomes easier. Pat's eager interest holds me accountable. As in life itself, I cannot do all the work alone.

I cannot create a healthy family by myself; I cannot make a friendship without another's participation; I cannot do the work of church or society in lonely isolation.

Pat's presence encourages me, cheers me on. Not only is my perennial garden growing well; but with nothing more than her encouragement, I've brought the herbal back door garden into shape, kept my Betty Prior rose bushes pest-free, curtailed the ambitious sedum in the rock garden, and started a cutting bed for drying flowers. I planted three hundred spring bulbs for naturalizing in the woods, and I am scheming about growth in every available inch of this suburban plot over which I am the priestess.

Ambitious? Perhaps.

But like Pat, I am eager to place this green sacrament into the hands of others so that in the communion of sharing, I too will have more.

16

The Co-Conspirators

I am a collector of perfect moments; these are the photos stored in the proof sheets of my memory, the ones I take out and hold in my palm . . . press the pad of my finger across their surfaces to enter briefly again into past time, into a few seconds when I knew a pure happiness buried in joy. For most of my life, these have been fleeting ecstasies enjoyed alone. Few people exult as intensively as I exult over the common and mysterious stuff of life. "Oh, look! Oh, look!" I cry. Unh-huh, they nod, and go back to reading their newspapers. Or they are embarrassed by me. I am over-wrought, they think. I have seen their sideways glances.

Still, I had an opportunity to store many such memories on the occasion of my daughter's wedding day. Weddings, in reality, are not always happy occasions for the people who plan them. Surviving a daughter's wedding is a rite of adult female passage. Having been a pastor's wife, party to more weddings than I can recollect, I had decided that there were some things I did not want to do. I did not want this event to become feminized with endless dinner-table conversations among the women concerning "The Wedding," which would bore male family members senseless. I would let go and let this be a Melissa Mains and Douglas Timberlake affair.

That meant they planned their own wedding—they did the shopping, they chose the invitations, and then they informed me of their decisions. My role was to facilitate their plans. A close friend, Jack Risley, a professional designer, assisted the young couple. They all, without me, went shopping for that informal look they were seeking. As far as I could tell, the "look" they had in mind mixed elements from the Great Gatsby era and an English country garden affair. Bridesmaids were to wear floral-patterned summer frocks. Tuxedos were nixed as too stuffy; the men were to be attired in white summer pants, white shoes, striped dress shirts, sleeveless knitted cotton vests and striped bow ties.

I even absented myself from shopping for the bride's gown. She was accompanied by her matron of honor — a close friend from high school days — by her friend's mother, and by her bridegroom-to-be. Doug, a theater major with training in set and costume design, knew about staging grand entrances, and since this was his wedding as much as Melissa's, why exclude him from the grand decisions? I entered the drama during Act II, when the final choice was made, and the costs had to be addressed.

Melissa and Douglas did as much as they could do to advance the August wedding plans before returning to Ohio to their summer jobs. Wisely, since I was also writing a book (appropriately enough on marriage), I accepted the offer of expertise from friends. An efficiency expert arranged the details of the reception. My sister, a degreed musician, contracted for the music: a woodwind ensemble to perform classical pieces for the ceremony, a harpist to provide quiet background for the reception, and a steel band to play reggae after dinner.

But I did reserve for myself the joy of indulging in a neglected passion. I decided that (with the help of my long-suffering friend Jack Risley) I would make all the wedding bouquets, the floral arrangements for the chapel, and the centerpieces for the reception. The idea was to raid friends' gardens for late summer flowers, mixing in as many roadside blooms and sprightly weeds as possible.

In order to do what you most want to do in life, other loves must be abandoned. I have imposed this harsh equation upon myself in order to write and concurrently raise four children. I used to be an eager student of art, roaming institutes and galleries. I used to restore abandoned furniture, spending hours stripping wasted finishes, getting slightly high on varnish remover, sanding, steel-wooling, staining anew the grains of fresh wood. I used to sew all my clothes. A deprived naturalist lurks in my soul; spring flowers, wildness, hidden fungi, the cry of migrating flocks—all these once gave me hours of solace. Not any longer, however; this list is a pathetic accumulation of some of the lesser loves I have sacrificed in order to develop the craft and discipline necessary to write.

So I decided I would give myself a gift for my daughter's wedding. I would give myself the joy again of floral arrangement. I remember standing in a farmer's field, two days before the Sunday ceremony, early, before seven o'clock, gathering buckets of wild parsnip, golden aster, purple coneflower, early goldenrod, heath aster, and wild snapdragon (popularly named butter-and-eggs). I held the bunches close, pressed the blooms against my face. Oh, thank you God, I whispered. *Thank you that this has been given back to me, and that I have time for these lovely things because of my daughter's wedding.*

Wendall Barry, in *The Gift of Good Land,* has written:

To live we must daily break the body and shed the blood of creation. When we do this knowingly, lovingly, skillfully and reverently, it is a sacrament. When we do it ignorantly, greedily, clumsily, and destructively, we condemn ourselves to spiritual moral loneliness and others to want.

I was breaking the pods and stems of creation, lovingly, in order to celebrate marriage. This was indeed a perfect moment. One might also call it sacramental, a time in which God's grace came to me through these actions.

Interestingly, my perfect moments are enhanced when chaos walks around the edge of the experience, when incongruity suddenly turns its wild mask on me. I delight when my serious purpose (my *too* serious purpose) is surprisingly turned topsy-turvy. We had no idea that this wedding summer would also be the time of the Midwest's Long Drought, a record string of rainless days stretching through the months, endless weeks in which the land was sucked dry by temperatures above 90 degrees. My perfect moment in that farmer's field was enhanced by the awareness that these hardy plants had stubbornly survived merciless aridity in order to lift head, stems, and pods to the glory of God, in order to be part of Melissa's wedding (of that I was maternally certain).

Jack and I had decided that on Friday before the Sunday wedding we would put together the fifteen centerpieces for the reception, the four oversized bouquets, two for either side of the front of the chapel and two for sideboards at the salad supper. They could be stored under the shade of the woods beside our yard and kept fresh with periodic mistings from the garden hose. I had already woven collected pods and dried statice into fourteen grapevine wreaths for the pew decorations, and splashed a white wash of paint on bridal wreaths for the chapel doors. All were wound with white and cream satin ribbons. Melissa's bouquet, long-stemmed white roses from the florist bunched with wild Queen Anne's lace, would be also tied with satin ribbons right before the ceremony and stored in the refrigerator. At the last minute I would combine herbs and flowers for the bridesmaids' baskets, casually arranged to look as though they had just been picked from the garden, which they would have been.

On returning home from my blissful moment in the farmer's field, I discovered Jack unloading armfuls of weeds from his car. He had brought a helper, his next-door neighbor, John. John is in his seventies, but has somehow retained the capacity for childlike inquiry. He accompanies my friend Jack to the grocery store and to designing jobs where he can act as an assistant. We dragged tables, containers, buckets, baskets, garbage pails into the backyard. No danger of rain today. I started on the centerpieces, and Jack began loading four huge vases with prairie dock, wild carrot, elderberry skeletons (the berries long gone as birds' victuals), great mullein, bergamot, joe-pye weed.

Jack kicked off his shoes, serious about this work. John followed him about, sustaining a rambling discourse of information and inquiry. "Shall I rake, Jack? Do you want water in these buckets? Do you want those flowers here? That's really looking good Jack! You do that great!"

Our neighbor's child, Mellicent, stayed pleasurably underfoot all morning. She brought the latest litter of kittens from the garage to the patio so she could keep an eye on them and on us. The gas station attendant, who needed a little more income, arrived to do the yardwork I feared would be neglected due to my manuscript deadline and the wedding. He brought his gangling yellow puppy, which for some reason wore a kerchief tied around its neck. "Cochise!" his master called as the dog scrambled through the yard. "Cochise!" The chain that dragged from his collar was toppling my flower buckets.

The early morning hours stretched to early afternoon. The bouquets were wild, untamed, like Jack and I liked them. Suddenly, I realized we hadn't had lunch. What on earth was in the refrigerator?

We all gathered around the center counter — one that had been rescued from a ramshackle farmhouse kitchen and now restored — and pulled up stools for Jack, John, Mellicent, and me. Let's see . . . oh, there were fresh blueberries.

We plumped them in four blue kitchen bowls. (Do you like blueberries, John? John liked blueberries. He told us how much he liked blueberries.) And there was an unsliced loaf of fresh homemade bread that had been dropped off by a friend. So we made a lunch of toasted wheat bread, blueberries with milk, and glasses of lemonade. Mellicent, usually so shy, climbed onto Jack's lap as he wrapped his bare feet around the four-legged stool.

This, I thought, this love feast is a perfect moment. Store it. Keep it. Wild things around me, plants and people. A backyard a' whacko with floral arrangements. Most women would consider me deranged, but, as I remember this scene, I am young again, gleeful with joy! Incongruity is here, chaos is near. A mongrel pup (wearing a kerchief) is scrambling around, tipping my centerpieces. Kittens chase each other in the dry grass. Watch out! Don't step on them! Something sacred is pausing for a moment. Here is a visitation.

It will never come again, this moment. It would deny replication. But I noticed its passing, touched its breastbone when it paused. Before we bowed our heads in greeting, we looked each other in the eye. I was not alone in the noticing; others had partaken of this epiphany. *Thanks be for gifts of shining time. Praises be for co-conspirators – creatures, growing things, strangers, friends. May I ever find others who love the visitations, who taste deeply of these secret joys.*

17

A Dancing Partner

Some of the strangers we encounter in life become our sons-
and daughters-in-law. For most of us, the people our children
marry are not the little boys and girls who used to play in
the backyard. We haven't watched them grow, nor attended
their piano recitals. They haven't been part of the park
district swim classes or summer league teams. We don't
know their families or their parents' professions. Our first
encounters come after that pivotal phone call, "Oh Mom,
Dad, there's someone I want you to meet."

I met Doug Timberlake during an after-performance party
in Oxford, Ohio, the town that hosts Miami University.
He and my daughter, Melissa, were both students in the
theatre department. Melissa asked me, in the way young
women do who need a trusted opinion but who don't want
to appear too interested: "So, what did you think of Doug
Timberlake?" Answers to these questions are exceedingly
crucial—beware! A parent can never be sure who will
become an in-law child.

I answered by saying that I liked Doug and felt that he
was a young man in search of a spiritual home. This is a

longing with which I am familiar, a yearning like that described by Wordsworth, ". . . hope that can never die / Effort, and expectation, and desire / And something evermore about to be." This is the mark of the artist, the mystic, the lost soul, and sometimes all three at once. It happens that I was right. Right now, Douglas is in the process of discovering his own spiritual terrain. His search has taken him into divinity studies at Asbury Theological Seminary. And he has, indeed, become my son-in-law.

Two years ago, at a Timberlake family wedding, I sat at the reception dinner table watching couples move onto the dance floor. How easy it all seemed! How appropriate to this festive passage. Did Christ dance at the wedding in Cana of Galilee? Perhaps there was longing in my eyes, but I noticed that Melissa nudged Doug and the next thing I knew, my son-in-law, handsome in his white tuxedo, was whispering, "How about this dance, Mom?"

I protested, "Douglas, I don't know how — I never learned. . . ." He laughed, took my hand, and drew me into the dancing couples. "It doesn't matter. No one will even know." And he was right, the dance floor was so crowded no one could see my stumble-footed two-step.

This invitation was deeply meaningful to me; a young man, my son-in-law, had included me in the dance. It was a gift of sorts, casually offered, which seemed to close some old wound. *Why had it been so special?* I wondered, driving home that night.

And why did the motif of a child's circle dance come up in my writing? It is a major symbol in my children's book *Tales of the Kingdom.* I have the painting for the book jacket, "The Great Celebration" — its subject, a sacred dance — displayed on an easel in my living room. There are also two other prints in the room, one an old classic of children in a joyous ring-around-the-rosy in a woods, and the other an etching of children dancing in a field of wildflowers outside a white country church.

114

I remembered how deeply moved I had been by the last scene in the film, *Babette's Feast,* which won the 1988 Academy Award for best foreign film. At the end of the film, old people dance in the moonlight around the town well, holding hands like children. There was something here, certainly—something needing to be understood.

I was raised in a religious subculture, fundamentalism, where dancing, smoking, the theatre, and cinema were expressly forbidden. One of my most embarrassing moments occurred at a junior high party to which I had been invited by a nonfundamentalist friend. I had been unaware there would be social dancing at the party (in her living room, with parents present, to rather subdued music as I recall). One of the boys, Dan Perry, asked me to dance. I was appalled. I could make one of two bad choices, either of which broke a familial code. I could refuse and offend the laws of hospitality (which were sacred to my father); or I could dance and offend the laws of morality (which were primary to my mother). I danced with the boy, but in such a confounded way, making comments about my partner's missteps, that even today I feel shame about the incident.

My shame has little to do with breaking my mother's moral code. This incident reminds me how I accepted and even championed an ethical system which was fraudulent to my own integrity.

I bought into a standard I didn't really believe in. Not only did I conform to the religious legal codes; I took this campaign against dance (especially social dance) as my own. To be safe, I refused party invitations which might place me in additional compromising situations. In eighth grade, I planned an all-city church youth banquet as a substitute for the junior-high spring dance. I carried endless notes from my mother asking for me to be excused from gym classes where my peers learned to square dance, while I sat alone in the library. In high school, I became the spokesperson to Student Council on the Christian prohibition against young

115

bodies touching in hothouses of lust as dance bands beat out their animal rhythms—in other words, I explained why we didn't attend sock hops. When modern dance sections were scheduled for physical education classes, I withstood my gym teacher's persuasive tactics (surprisingly intense as I consider them now). I suggested an alternate section for those of us who refrained due to religious convictions. We withdrew from the gym to the equipment room and practiced jump roping, which we exhibited later, at a spring program where the modern dance class performed their routines.

In a way, this was tragic. Some of my more iconoclastic Christian friends eventually rebelled against this kind of religion, throwing out the faith as well as the legalism. If my lovely and most well-meaning mother had simply said, "Karen, this is a prohibition to which I subscribe, and I'm asking you to conform until you are an adult and can make your own decision," I might have conformed without paying such a high emotional price. Instead, I was manipulated into making a decision which supposedly represented my deep religious convictions. Actually, I had very little choice. I would have been emotionally excommunicated by the elders of my religious community if I had blatantly appeared at the Spring Prom. (The bogeyman of abandonment often crops up in situations where we are manipulated, through fear, into deceiving ourselves about who we really are.)

The tragedy for me was that I lived the lie; for at heart, I am a balletomane. I love the dance and dancing. It is an outward expression of the things I feel going on in my soul. The dance floor was off limits to me, not because of my own hard-won beliefs, but because someone else's anxiety had been imposed upon me. And a part of me—a hidden part of me—knew it. This led to the making of a hypocrite.

My own children have been raised by a much more exacting code—the rule of love, daily obedience to the Holy Spirit, and inner-purity—which may or may not have anything to do with whether they dance. That has been a decision left to their own devising. They all go to the theater (circumspectly), follow the movies (discriminately), attend and give dances. They prove to me how ridiculous some of these human standards were. All four of these children deeply love the Lord, and amaze me with how they live out their Christian faith in their aggressively secular worlds.

I remember when David and I dropped one of the boys off at a junior high dance. The pubescent girls were huddled together in a tight cluster on the north side of the lawn, their party dresses forming one quivering pastel flower, petals crushed together, with multi-leg stems sticking to the ground, ankles collapsing in their new high heels as if on cue. The pubescent boys, alternately, were clumped together on the south side of the lawn. They hovered about, awkward in their new suits and starched white shirts. "And this," I said to my husband, "is what our parents were protecting us from?"

Dance is a language. And just as the language with which we are most familiar, the spoken word, can be used for good or ill—as a means of knowing God or, through its misuse, as a means of alienating ourselves from God—so dance has its own range of uses, from worship to illicit eroticism. We don't stop speaking because we might find ourselves cursing or lying (and who among us has never lied?); so why should we not dance just because dancing can be abused?

Admittedly, the simple action of joining hands and dancing around in a circle can be either a child's game of ring-around-the-rosy or part of a witches' coven's infernal rite. But the same statement, "Christ, the King of the Jews," can be either a confession of Christian faith or Pilate's self-damning admission. The Lord looks on the heart. It is the way we use languages that matters, not the languages themselves.

During my legalistic past my spirit suffered from inhibitions of artistic expression of which dance is a symbol. My soul is a dancing creature. That inward rhythm needed an outward bodily action, a physical reaching, symbolic of spiritual celebration. Hippolytus in the third century wrote, "This is the paschal feast. . . . This feast of the Spirit leads the mystic dance through the year."

When God comes among us, when we recognize his presence, we need to give expression or testimony with all our being. For some that is words, for some that is song, for some that is silence or prayer, for some that is laughter or tears, for some that is poetry. There are many languages in which we express what we feel. Rigidity diminishes what we include in worship and is liable to diminish what we feel in our hearts. It was the blacks of the sixties and seventies, those who came to our church in the city, who taught me that sometimes "what you gotta do is dance in the aisles." Gregory Thaumaturgous, a third-century Christian missionary, expressed it well, "Dance with me, Jordan River, and leap with me, and set your waves in rhythm, for your Maker has come to you in body!"

So I will bless the dance, especially the folk dances that speak of a world of people — God's children, the Italian pavane, the German's sprightly allemande, Spain's passionate saraband or the chaconne, the wondrous English country-dance.

And I will praise God for the strangers my children bring home who become my dancing partners; for the one who speaks the laughing words, "it doesn't matter," and who takes my hand and leads me back to the dance floor. I realize he is right — it doesn't matter, not any longer. For God is my true dancing partner, and I am finally able to join Him in His dance.

18

The Rumtopf *Maker*

The memories I have of Sherline Dunkerton are like the dessert topping *rumtopf*. To make a starter of *rumtopf* you mix one cup of dried and fresh fruit, one cup of sugar, and one-quarter cup rum. These ingredients are left to ferment in the back of the refrigerator. For every cup of the rich mixture spooned out, you add more fruit and sugar and rum and you stir it every so often so that the sweet chunky marinade keeps replenishing itself in its jar. Like *rumtopf,* my experiences with Sherline seem to keep brewing a savory concoction.

Tom and Sherline were strangers when the invitation came for David to preach in their church in Briarcliff Manor, Westchester County, in New York State. At the Dunkertons' request, we packed four grade-school kids into a car, drove cross-country, and plunked the family entourage into a household of complete strangers. The enticements the Dunkertons had offered included free housing, meals, and guided tours of New York City. Our inner-city pastorate and a decidedly limited vacation budget contributed much to our audacious acquiescence.

We were greeted with the same expansiveness which became a hallmark of the many future times we were to come together, mostly at the Dunkertons' invitation. Right away, in that first visit, one of our boys bloomed with the rash of three-day measles. This hitch in our plans didn't bump Sherline's schedule one whit. She orchestrated Staten Island Ferry rides, trips to the Statue of Liberty, menus, babysitting, transport—and did everything with wonderful enthusiasm.

I have been in Tom and Sherline's home many times since and have never come away with anything less than rich, sustaining memories. I was a stranger and they took me, us—all of us—in. Sherline is one of the few friends I have who delights more deeply in the moment than I do myself. She sucks the marrow out of the bone, and she does this so unselfishly that all within her parameter are invited to rejoice with her on life's wild ride.

Sherline doesn't impress you right away as a woman of the world. She is comfortable in waistless dresses that hang in gathers from a yoke, hiding her extra weight. She pads impatiently on flat, sensible shoes to get where she is going. Through the years her salt and pepper hair has grown into a ring of grey that frames her face. Her eyes are alive, often tender; her laugh gentle, conveying care. One prestigious friend, handsome and dark-haired—married to an equally attractive, exceedingly trim wife (his goal, he said, was to pamper her)—turned and within my hearing said, wistfully: "Sherline, if I get sick, will you come take care of me?"

My *rumtopf* memories include a wintry morning at The Metropolitan Museum of Art where forced cherry blossoms bloomed from magnificent jardinieres in niches in the lobby. Here the lavish blossoms of Van Gogh's irises were on exhibit. We spent several hours studying these great works.

Afterward, Sherline and I sloshed across Fifth Avenue, soaking our shoes in the curbside snow mash. We stopped to eat lunch in a chic restaurant, where I removed my sodden stockings, spread them (as inconspicuously as possible) on a radiator nearby, and sat on my numb bare feet. You can do these kinds of inappropriate things with Sherline. She doesn't tsk-tsk. If you wish, you can even press the glad unshod soles of your feet to the New York pavement and dance out the mazurka pounding in your heart. Sherline never thinks you a fool for this gladness.

Into our *rumtopf* memories she mixed an Emil Gilel piano recital at Carnegie Hall and the discovery of Zabar's delicatessen. One time she added Jason Robards and Colleen Dewhurst in Eugene O'Neill's *A Moon for the Misbegotten.* She stirred in Natalia Makarova's dancing figure at the Lincoln Center where the audience booed the orchestra and gave the ballerina a standing ovation. She measured out Tiffany's, where the only thing I could afford were a few tiny Elsa Peretti lopsided hearts on silver chains as gifts for my daughter and friends. The *rumtopf* juices of these memories soak together, distilling a sweet savor.

Sherline has given me many perfect days. Notes from July 1976 read: "Bookstores in the morning. Shakespeare at Delacorte Theatre in Central Park in the evening. Stood in a long line behind hundreds, all who waited for passes to gain tickets for admission. Many brought picnic dinners, bottles of *vin rosé.* Balding young executive in suit met his wife in front of us; she was wearing dungarees and a bold blue and white striped shirt. He held his attaché case; she carried a rattan picnic basket. Wonderful conversation: 'What is Jews for Jesus? They're all over town.'

"'I guess they're Jews who like Jesus.'

"'How can they like Jesus and be Jews?'

"The line snaked through the late-afternoon sunshine toward the theatre, past an instrumental ensemble—a marimba, a violin, and a baritone horn. Wandering minstrels, dressed in purple, honored all those who weren't wearing leather shoes. Foreign exchange students from Brazil danced in the line ahead of us, clicking their empty pop cans in Latin rhythms; they sang, 'Brasilia! Brasilia!' We grabbed the last two tickets, then Tom and Sherline and their daughter Betsy waited by the gate (in case some ticketholders didn't show). David and I went in and seated ourselves, hoping the others would follow. Vendors sold cold apple juice, nut and raisin trail mix, fresh fruit, and slices of French bread; calling out, 'Outrageously delicious homemade brownies!'

"Tom and Sherline and Betsy got the last three tickets in the [no-show] waiting line! Meanwhile, the foreign exchange students chanted antiphonal cheers back and forth across the open-aired theatre. An irate man headed up the aisle and hushed them with, 'This is not the proper behavior. This is a *theatah!*' When he had gone, I turned and told those seated behind me that I admired their spirit (after all, they'd been dancing for at least two hours!) but that some people took their *pre-performance* Shakespeare very seriously.

"*Henry V,* a Joseph Papp production, starring Paul Rudd as Henry and [the then unknown] Meryl Streep as Katherine, was glorious on the open stage. Banners floated in the real wind behind a huge cast in striking, stylized battle scenes. Now and then, a dipping helicopter overhead drowned out actors' lines. Echos thrust stiletto sound across the lagoon. The skyline began to twinkle as late afternoon gave way to early evening and then yielded to night—a lively backdrop behind the stage.

"We left repeating lines from the play to each other '. . . we few, we happy few, we band of brothers. For he today that sheds his blood with me shall be my brother. . . .' Walking home through Central Park past policeman posted beneath shining globe lamps, we were a happy band of brothers, secure with one another, and very wealthy."

"*Il n'y a pas de vie heureuse; il y a seulement des jours heureux*" is a French expression that means: "There is no happy life; there are only happy days." But when we learn to recognize the potential sacrament of the present moment, that God can be here in this now, in this unexpected pleasure, then the possibility of living happily emerges. A line from the hymn "Jesus, Thou Joy of Loving Hearts" reads, "make every moment calm and bright." Sherline has given me bright moments. I will never come to the end of her rich *rumtopf*. The more I stir, the more fragrantly it bubbles, this fruity stew fermenting in its own tasty juices.

I try to remember the meaning of a life like Sherline's at all times, not only when I am threatened with its loss. Words must be spoken, love given now; opportunities evaporate like mists above a marsh in a wind. That becomes even more clear when I receive the kind of news we have just had from Tom. Our friend Sherline has cancer, and she will have to undergo chemotherapy.

I am a woman who sucks out the marrow of life as well. I do not want any of it to pass me by. I am lusty in my desire for its bright moments. I do not want to watch the crowds. I want to be padding along in the midst of the mob. Give me chance encounters on street corners. Let me hear the catcalls of the construction workers. When I laugh, let me have my hearty howl, let me throw back my head and stamp my foot. Let people say, "I knew you were here, I heard you laughing." I want to feel the pain as deeply as I can bear it. I want the exultation to be as wild as inhibitions will allow. I don't want artificiality. I want to be where it's dangerous to be, an adventuress chasing risk and riot.

Too many cautious friends, too many acquaintances preoccupied with their mission in the world, too many proper theologians in my life leave me feeling like a bewildered child being punished at the state fair—kept by some punitive relative from sampling the delights at the gaming booths, the exhibit barns, the home shows. Why do I feel like I have escaped when I am with Sherline? Escaped from what?

If asked to describe herself, Sherline would probably say that she was just a homemaker, Tom's wife, a mother, and a grandmother. She would not classify herself as one of those people who fills her space in the world exceptionally well.

But she does, she does! Not just for me, but for all who know her. The very thought of Sherline Dunkerton gives me comfort. Her exquisite delight—in the birds on the feeder, in the people at her door, in all things strange and remarkable, all things bright and marvelous—is her blessing, the secret ingredient to this *rumtopf* she habitually concocts.

When next I go to New York City, I will buy a twisted Elsa Peretti heart like the one Sherline wears, but smaller; not to give away but to wear close, resting against my skin and warming between my breasts—a reminder to celebrate the extravagant gifts that strangers can bring, one of which may be the rare charity of friendship. And I will think of Sherline Dunkerton, the woman who helped me escape in New York City.

19

Long-Lost Brother

In the modernization of the Camelot story *The Once and Future King* by T. H. White, the author states that King Arthur originated one new idea every ten years. I myself have an idea that has been a decade in the making. If someone were to inquire—"Can a Christian man and woman be friends?"—after ten years of consideration, I would say yes.

This thought represents a concept so revolutionary it compares to King Arthur's proposition that law should rule instead of might. This concept has to do with the war between the sexes—including the ecclesiastical war between the sexes—and is hardly original to me. Rather, Paul developed this idea, and he assimilated it from Christ, a true revolutionary in all things.

This thinking began during a journey overseas when a man popped into the foreign office on my first day up-country. Blond and trim and tall, with a crooked grin, he wore the usual khaki safari suit of field-staff relief workers, which often renders attractive men even more handsome. Properly chaperoned by a party of six people, but unaccompanied by our spouses, we traveled together for ten days. The trip thrust us into exotic locales and the drama of refugee camps. We shared hilarious adventures, met strange and courageous folk, enjoyed hours of conversation, and in the course of those ten days, we became friends. When I examined my feelings for this man, I realized I felt comfortable, as though I had discovered a long-lost brother. And I was glad, so glad.

I believe that Christian men and women can be friends. I have come to the conclusion that there is an unusual spiritual power released into the world by holy cross-gender friendships. I believe Christ came to establish a new order of human relationships which was part of His original design for His children here on earth. This is some of what He was attempting to teach when He said in Mark, "Who are my mother and my brothers! Whoever does the will of God is my brother, and sister, and mother."

Now I am aware of the war between the sexes. Having written a book, *Child Sexual Abuse*, I know about the depravity of the human heart. I have heard countless stories from women of sexual seduction by missionary grandfathers, church elders, pastors, and youth workers. On the other hand, I also know that men have been damaged by the women in their lives, non-nurturing or domineering mothers, man-eating females, seductive choir directoresses. This pitched battle has been raging for centuries. It is one of the hostilities Christ died to cure.

My trip overseas followed hard upon the heels of a two-year discussion in our former church about whether women could be elders. I had been invited to take part in this dialogue and to function as an elder—sort of on trial. I realized now that in these many-times bitter negotiations, I was the victim of one man's misogyny, which he turned into his own peculiar brand of theology. So it was good to travel with a gentle brother with a crooked grin; a man who had a shy, soft-spoken manner when he gave me compliments—compliments that never left me wondering if he was angling for something else.

Paul writes about the redemptive principle of charity breaking down false divisions, which he applies to the warfare between Jews and Gentiles: "For Christ himself is our way of peace. . . . By his death he ended the angry resentment between us, . . . As parts of the same body, our anger against each other has disappeared, for both of us have been reconciled to God. And so the feud ended at last at the cross" (Ephesians 2:14-16, TLB). This reconciliation should also be applied to the sexes.

Instructions about Christ's new order (or perhaps we should say, the Edenic order that was destroyed because of disobedience) are more specifically included in Paul's counsel to young Timothy, "Never speak sharply to an older man, but plead with him respectfully just as though he were your own father. Talk to the younger men as you would to much loved brothers. Treat the older women as mothers, and the girls as your sisters, thinking only pure thoughts about them" (1 Timothy 5:1-2, TLB). This, of course, can be reversed sexually: "Treat the older men as fathers, and the boys as your brothers, thinking only pure thoughts about them."

If this injunction were followed in our churches, we would change our society. This is a society where, for the most part, men know only how to use women, control them, or possess them; where women manipulate men. Intimacy seems possible only in the sex act. Men and women are starving for healing between the sexes, which is why they keep seeking it in inappropriate and ultimately destructive sexual liaisons.

Unfortunately, Christians have not forged a Christ-like peace; we have become compulsively protective, reactionary. Women must be kept in their places. Men and women must not become too friendly. If you are married, fidelity requires you to keep yourself so much unto your spouse that only superficial relationships with other men or women are allowed. ("And no wonder we are rigid," some might object, "when so many of our leaders fall prey to infidelity, promiscuity, and sexual addiction." "And no wonder so many of them fall prey when we are so unnatural," I reply.)

There's a better way a few of us with strength enough, with wisdom enough, must forge. In fact, I would like to state boldly that some of my best friends are Christian men. Some have been in small groups with me, some I have met in travels, some are professional colleagues, some hold me accountable for my own spiritual growth, some are younger, some are older, some are my age. Not one of these friendships has been sexualized in any way (by that I mean, no fondling, no flirting, no stolen caresses, no dishonest appointments). Yet we are free to touch, to embrace in passing, to give a peck on the cheek, to share human feelings and struggles. In short, we are discovering what it means to be part of Christ's new order, brothers and sisters in a spiritual family, a confederacy of holiness.

Unfortunately, the conservative Protestant community in its caution creates the very vacuum that sucks men and women into a black hole of uniformly sexual relationships. The truth is that we are lonely for each other because we were created to need each other. "I wish I had one good male friend," I often hear women say. "I wish there were some women I could trust, with whom to discuss this," men say. Spouses cannot meet all of each other's needs. Single adults need complementary cross-gender friendships.

There are rules that must be followed. The first rule is that we must not withhold Christ-like love from one another. The second rule is that our relationships, outside the married relationship, must not be sexualized in any way.

In history there have been many spiritual friendships between the sexes that have followed these rules. One of the most celebrated is the story of Francis of Assisi and Clare.

Clare was fourteen when the reputation of the son of Pietro Bernardone reached her ears: he had withdrawn from the commerce of the secular world, established his order of Poor Brothers, had changed his hermit's garb for that of a

128

barefoot preacher, and restored the several crumbling churches in the vicinity with stones begged in the city. He lived with and nursed the lepers on the plain below Assisi.

Soon she heard him preach; she heard him deliver his prophet's message of love that reformed the times.

When Clare was eighteen, she left the world, formed the Poor Sisters, and lived in a cloister—an enclosed world—like other nuns of her era. She loved Francis, and Francis loved her ("Do not believe," he said, "that I do not love her with a perfect love"); and they used this love to refuel their own burning desire for God. One writer has said that "between them they invigorated not only Italy but also Christian Europe. They kindled a new poetry, a new art, a renewed religion."

Reconciliation, certainly, is the will of God; reconciliation between men and men, between races, between warring parties of the true church, between men and women. (Who are my brothers and my sisters? Those who do the will of God.)

The stranger I met on a trip far from home was a brother. We walked on a Mediterranean beach in the moonlight, talking about the physical and emotional loss of our fathers. We flew from one backwater of civilization to another in small planes, bumped along in the Land Rover out to tribal territory (where tribal elders gave us a live kid goat as a gift), and climbed over mountainous terrain on foot (and brought back spears and machetes for our children). He complimented me by guessing that I was six years younger than I am (an open sesame to my good favor), and protected me from the flirtations of a national government tour guide.

He protested against the necessity of all men going through a mid-life crisis. I insisted that he was protesting too much, and asked, wasn't he, in fact, in a mid-life crisis of his own? We got marooned (with our accompanying party) in an off-beat hotel in a foreign city when the planes for the next leg of our journey didn't arrive, ate the same dinner

129

three nights running (all that was offered on the menu), listened to a concert of pitiful renditions of American rock music. We talked about our childhoods, how we became Christians, our spiritual aspirations, our likes and dislikes, told the most embarrassing, the most riotous, the most dreadful moments of our life stories; explained why we loved our spouses and what needed changing in our marriages.

When I returned home, he called me from far away and said, "Thank you for loving me. I've gone ahead and started therapy." And I began to consider the question, *Can Christian men and women become friends?* A consideration which, like King Arthur's idea, has taken me ten years to examine.

In the process I uncovered pockets of hatred toward some men in my own heart, confessed my error, asked for forgiveness, mended my ways.

Then I discovered that I am lonely for my brothers, I am lonely for this lost half of my female self. I want reconciliation. I am weary of this dividing wall of hostility Christ my Brother came to tear down. I want to put away the world's ways, this damaging civil war of the sexes that rips apart our spiritual union.

In ten years of thinking and praying, I have decided that men and women in Christ can be friends—we can have cross-gender friendships—but that only a few have the courage and the holiness to love each other in such a way that the world is invigorated.

20

Jack-Of-All-Trades

Thirteen years ago, within twelve months of moving into our home, we began to have problems with water damage. First the dormers in the front bedrooms leaked when there were hard rains. Then, during a winter of record-breaking snowfalls, the snow on the roof froze hard, impacting the ice-line, which turned to water within the attic when the ice met the warm air rising from inside the house. This resulted in some twenty different dripping leaks through the living room and dining room ceilings.

Insurance, of course, paid for this water damage, but the money went to pay a tuition bill that was also due.

Then the pipes in one of the upstairs bathrooms froze and a child (who shall remain nameless) unintentionally left his dry water faucet in the "on" position. When we returned from church that Sunday afternoon, the pipes had thawed. Water gushed over the sink, rushed along the floorboards, fell like a waterfall in the dining room, and then seeped down into the basement.

Later, a crack in the foundation resulted in water collecting in the northeast corner of the basement. When a sump

131

pump gave out during spring storms, when the humidifier on the furnace went, when the drain in the laundry room sink plugged and overflowed during the washing machine spin cycles, more water collected—a lot more water. All of this water stained an indelible water line on the new rough cedar siding.

Why didn't we have all this fixed?

In self-defense, I can say that I have called plumbers. I've pleaded with roofmen. Every one of them told me something must be done. All looked at the bows and waves in the plasterboard and said, "Lady, you're going to have to replace that whole ceiling before it tears off and falls on someone's head." But then they just disappeared, never to be heard of again.

And truthfully, between tithes, taxes, and college tuitions, there just didn't seem to be enough money to go around so I didn't insist they return to do the work.

The leaks in my house have amounted to domestic Chinese water torture. I've prayed for years, tried to resign myself to the mess, looked in the other direction, but finally, on December 1, 1989, I was a discouraged lady.

I know this because I recorded my feelings in my prayer journal. "Friday, December 1, 1989," I wrote. "A bad day. Feeling emotionally discouraged."

Actually, I had had a bad year. The year 1989 had brought discouraging news to many para-church ministries, our national broadcast, "The Chapel of the Air," included. Mail response, partly as a result of the televangelist scandals, had dropped drastically. Never before had we suffered such financial reversals. (And that is saying something, because The Chapel has rarely, underline *rarely*, been anything more than solvent.) David had been forced to cut $400,000 out of an already-trimmed 1990 budget. We dropped stations not paying for their own air time in financially stricken areas of the country, released long-term employees, repositioned our entire work force in an attempt to cover responsibilities.

We spent hours in prayer and days in fasting seeking the comfort and leading of the Lord.

Keeping vigil over a ministry in what might be its death throes (and with the only words from the Lord regarding the future being "Trust me") forces painful self-questioning upon the ministry's leaders. And on Friday, December 1, 1989, I was weary of hoping, weary of fighting off anxiety, exhausted from self-examination, and dumbfounded as to how to pray. ("All prayed-out!" is a family expression that described my state.) Despite my Christian walk, I was simply unable to trust that the Lord Almighty was doing His good work in our lives.

What did I want? I asked myself. Not very much. I just wanted enough financial bread for each day for The Chapel of the Air year. I didn't need us to be contenders for the largest, most successful media ministry. I didn't expect broad and rapid expansion of listener outlets. I didn't want the newest, biggest buildings, or state-of-the-art recording studios. I just wanted enough to pay this day's bills and make up the horrendous debt, some $750,000 worth, which had accumulated since the scandal-filled summer of 1989.

Oh, it was a bad day that first day of December. My journal records four more short items of "what I wanted." The last reads: "I'd be perfectly content with my personal material life if only the leaks in the ceilings of our home were repaired." In more candid terms that meant: "And oh, by the way, God, if You're so great; if You've promised to take care of all our needs, why don't You do something simple. Fix the leaks in the ceiling, for instance! I've been praying about that a long time."

Miraculously (and I mean that), by December 22, 1989, the living room and dining room ceilings had been torn out, the leaks located and repaired, and new plasterboard mounted and taped. How did all this happen?

A young man we had never met, a pastor who had just resigned and was between jobs, walked into David's office and said: "I don't have funds to help you in your financial crisis, but I know I wouldn't have made it through this last year without your radio broadcast. I do have construction skills. Is there anything I can do along that line?"

And like the Little Red Hen, he did. He surveyed our house, sighed, then took on the largest, messiest, most difficult of the neglected jobs. He carried out the furniture to the garage or stacked it in the bedrooms. He unfastened the chandelier from its electrical connection, ripped out the moldering dry wall, removed toilets (and since they were out, replaced them), tore up the flooring in the bathroom, located leaks, repaired leaks, laid new tile of my choice, grouted the tubs, and mounted fresh plasterboard.

All this for a grand total of $234.31. My benefactor wrote my bill out on stationery imprinted with a heading that read:

JACK-OF-ALL-TRADES
General Home Repairs
Painting, Carpentry, Plumbing, Roofing

His charges were for materials. His labor: $00.00.

Let us not investigate the peculiar theology of an angry, discouraged woman before her God. Let me instead praise the great gift this young man gave to me. First of all, there was the work, the repair itself; David and I could never have afforded to pay for this labor. As needful as it was, it was beyond our financial means. That was the obvious gift.

But just as the drip damage was a symbol of our greater problem—a ministry leaking away thousands upon thousands of dollars—the act of this man accumulated deeper levels of meaning for me.

David is not a Mr. Fix-it. He grew up in a family that hired out household repairs. In my family, my dad (when he could get around to it) fixed everything from cars to sinks to washing machines.

This was wonderful to me. It established in my mind the idea: *Dad can take care of it.* When he found time from his duties as the head of the Music Department at Moody Bible Institute, Dad would make it right. (The shadow of this is that we had four castoff automatic washers collected in the basement for extra parts—just in case.) One of the wonderful experiences of my childhood was watching Dad make things work. Sometimes, we children were invited to help him.

One of my dad's favorite do-it-yourself measures solved the problem of clogged drains. He would run a garden hose from the outside spigot through an open window into the house, plunge it down the clogged drain, turn on the pressure, and flush out the line.

He was a sublimely pragmatic handyman. Once, the line from the outside sewer backed up, gnarled with tree roots. This required that we rent an electric router from a nearby plumbing supply. Dad lifted the sewer cap and started to use the router, but he found that the line didn't slip into the L in the pipe going out to the street. So Dad lowered me—wrists clasped to wrists—down into the sewer where I could feed the line into the sewer conduit, taking the play out of the twisting contraption.

When a parent is alive who can make things work, a child feels as though chaos can be kept at bay. My father always calmed me by beginning his explanations with, "Now Sweet . . . now Sweet, what seems to be the trouble?"

After his death I felt his loss in many ways, and one of them was most certainly his absence in times of minor domestic crises. There was no one to be a father to me now. No one to make it work, to know how to fix it. No one to call and whine, "Dad, this stupid sink's backed up again!" Or, "The boys flushed their plastic soldiers down the toilets!"

Jack-Of-All-Trades could do the things my dad had been able to do. His help made me feel that I was cared for, protected. He could even pass on the wisdom of carpentry and tools to my children. My third son, Joel, was home on his winter break from college when Jack-Of-All-Trades tore out my ceiling. For much of the time, they worked in tandem. See, this is the way you remove a toilet. This is the way you use a cordless drill. This is the way you lay a sub-floor. This is the way you drop a plumb line. This is the way you measure out tile. This is how you put up dry wall. This is how you tape, prime, and paint a new ceiling. Unasked-for gifts now given.

Most importantly, this gift of a stranger put me back to rights again with my God. I understood very clearly by the timing of this answer to prayer, that the divine Mr. Fix-it—upon whom I was more obviously forced to depend after the death of my father—was saying: *Now Sweet, now Sweet, what seems to be the matter? I am perfectly able to answer your prayers in ways that are unfathomable to you. But the timing must be mine. When the time is right and when the way is right, I can bring all things about. And that is the fixing I most deeply needed.*

21

Friends Again

Recreating the past is like undertaking an impressionistic painting by committee. My brother, Craig, and I recently attempted to recall events from his childhood. (Let's see, Mother went to work when you were around two . . .) Struggling to overcome some anxieties, he felt he needed to understand their possible source. But we found establishing the truth of what-happened-when hard going. The past, at best, is a passionate observation, warped by emotions, skewed by personal perspective, and always, always, an unfinished work.

We had to go at this task alone without the guidance of an older generation—without the guidance of the people who knew these things as adults, rather than the way we knew them as children—because our parents had passed away some years before. They died during the decade of my thirties and during the decade of my brother's twenties. So we were left without masters, without those who might illumine the way it was. Without those who would have been in a position to comment, "When you were little, you said. . . ." Or, "I remember your first grade teacher. Daddy told you how pretty she was, and the next day you repeated. . . ." Or, "Remember when. . . ." There was no older generation to illustrate technique, to show us how to contrast light and shadow—no one to daub bright bursts of color in this abstract work called remembering.

So with two different brushstyles (my brother's delicate, fine-lined; mine bold, thick-stroked) and different palettes (his monochromatic, quiet in tone; mine primary, forthright) my brother and I recreated a fragment of the past. Much white space still remained on the canvas, certain areas were untouched, there was nothing at all around the borders.

Without a "remember-when" generation, vaguely familiar sounds, phrases I seem to have heard before, tricky dates, all haunt me. "I have been here before," the poet writes. "But when or how I cannot tell: / I know the grass beyond the door, / The sweet keen smell, / The sighing sound, the lights around the shore . . ." [Dante Gabriel Rossetti].

For instance, after a strenuous weekend of activity at my local church, I woke Monday morning reluctant to drag myself from bed. *That church has wore me all out,* I kept thinking to myself, *that church has wore me all out.* The fractured grammar teased my memory. Where had I heard it before?

Suddenly, I remembered a story—a story my mother used to tell. When I was a little girl, my father and I used to engage in wild roughhousing which we dubbed "ruffling." "Let's ruffle," I would challenge. My memory of these raucous tumbling sessions in our third floor apartment off Logan Boulevard in Chicago have an audio accompaniment. It is my mother's voice, "Dick! Dick! Not so rough," she would cry. "You'll hurt her. You'll hurt her!"

This never gave the two of us much pause. The rule was: if I wept, the ruffling ended. Consequently, I choked back my cries when my cheeks were rubbed raw by Father's rough-whiskered skin.

One time, as the story goes, my father called it quits. A guest in our home, a family friend, questioned me, "What's wrong with your father?" and I replied, "Oh, I wore he all out. I wore he all out."

So there it is, the source of my unbidden memory on that ragged Monday morning. But I had no one to phone, no one to whom I could say: "Mother, I just remembered that funny story you used to tell. Who was the family friend? And how old was I? And why did Dad and I roughhouse so wildly?" At that moment I missed her painfully.

I realized, once again, how incomplete I felt without her next to me, and I wondered whether I might ever reclaim what she had meant to me. For right then, years after her death, I was in the process of defining myself as an individual apart from her influence.

It wasn't until after my mother's death — she died on my thirty-ninth birthday — that I began to examine where the personality of Wilma Burton ended and the personality of Karen Mains began. This struggle should occur in adolescence and our young adult years, but mine was delayed by the "enmeshment" — an unhealthy closeness — in our relationship.

My "individuation" was complicated by grief. I needed to separate, to distinguish where her voice ended and my own unique self began. In parting one's self from a dead parent, one often negates the parent's influence in ways necessary to the maturing process while at the same time longing for the parent's presence. The two difficult emotional journeys traveled hand in hand. I would remember the unhealthy ways mother had lived her life through me, then suddenly long for her presence as during family celebrations.

When my first son was married, I decided to prepare the rehearsal dinner in my kitchen, then transport the meal to our rented reception hall. I spent the morning slicing cold beef, dipping it in marinade, and wiping tears. I wanted my mother by my side, missed her joy in this first grandson's marriage, yearned for the mother and daughter gossip we might have shared.

This emotional seesawing went on for years. And sometimes, frankly, I resented that in my forties, I was doing the work of an adolescent while raising adolescents myself. Mothers should assist their fledglings out of the nest; mine kept me too close, and at times I felt angry because of it.

One day, however, seven years after mother's death, as I was rummaging through the files we had stored in a walk-in closet, I discovered an unpublished article written by my mother which I had never read. The article is a humorous recalling of a week some twelve years ago in which Grandma Dobbie (as my children had dubbed her) had taken care of my four kids while I was off on a business trip in California. Reading her words, hearing fragments of her voice (so melodious, so wondrously soothing) in my ear, I dropped to the floor of the walk-in closet and began to laugh with an unaccountable sense of relief. I could see the ironic expression in mother's eyes. I remembered her suppressed grin.

The article shows that my mother did reasonably well keeping up with the school schedules of four children. She refers to my instructions magnetized on the refrigerator door. "Melissa leaves for school at 7:00; Randy at 7:30; Joel and Jeremy at 8:30." She figured out the cross-references on the back hall bulletin board regarding orthodontist appointments and music lessons. She made alternate arrangements, with considerable aplomb, when she was supposed to be in two places at once. She dealt well with the after-school clamor, the minor crises of children, with friends coming and going, phone calls, and with my phone counselees.

She reports on chasing down the two dogs who slipped out the back door when she took out the garbage:

> "Don't let them go near Sam," Jeremy cautions me.
> "Who's Sam?"
> "He's the husky next door."
> I can see a white shadow menacing the bushes on the far side of the lot. So that's where all the barking is coming from.

"Sam's the reason Narnia had puppies and mother won't let the dogs go over there any more."

She writes about the dinner hour:

Punctual son-in-law David walks in at 5:20 and says, "Boy, does it smell good in here!" Seated around the table, the boys promptly announce they can't stand peas, they can't stand deviled eggs, they can't stand salad. I tell them I can only stand for one "I-can't-stand" at a meal. Joel, eight years old, settles for not standing the eggs. He takes one pea on his plate. Jeremy, six years of age, imitates his brother's example.

Now those of us who have raised children know this is all standard stuff. My mother successfully reared three offspring to adulthood. She may have temporarily forgotten some of the chaos, but it was not new.

Where she did find difficulty was with our family pets— one dog with two puppies, one dog with puppies on the way, two hamsters, plus one basement containing several hundred fish swimming in four aquariums. She quotes from my instructions on the refrigerator door under the category, "Dogs."

Have children take them out. Narnia (the West Highland terrier) is to be watched and called in. Portia (the cocker spaniel) is to be put on chain. Do this early morning, noon, after school, after dinner, before bed. Make sure Portia sleeps downstairs in the laundry room. Narnia must stay with her pups in the bathtub in my bathroom. Portia will probably deliver while you are there. Instructions are in the dog books. Good luck. Try and make birthing chamber in the laundry room.

Mother's article continues:

"See, Dobbie," Randy (the high school freshman) says, holding the dog books in his hand, "Portia is panting. That's the way Narnia did before she delivered."

Happily for me the week ended with no birthing. Karen returned from her California trip glowing.

Two days back home, on a Sunday afternoon, Melissa calls me to say Portia is having her pups, and will I come help with the birthing since her parents are gone for a drive. Foolish woman, I say to myself as I back the car from the drive, chastising my soft heart. Foolish, foolish woman.

Missy has made a "birthing chamber" consisting of one old blanket in her room. One puppy is already born. Deep chocolate in color with a white vest. "Isn't he darling?" Melissa asks me. I want to say, "Yes, in a rat-like way," but am interrupted by the arrival of a black pup. Missy exclaims, "Oh, he's just like Portia!"

The parents return after the third pup is born, and I decline Missy's invitation to spend the night. As I enter the door, the phone rings. Missy. "The fourth one has just come. It's black and white."

I had prophesied five puppies. But morning brings another phone call and the announcement from Karen whose voice sounds weary, "Portia's had four more pups during the night. Nine pups in all — and I never saw such a motley lot! Melissa's asleep. She'll probably sleep until noon."

My hairdresser is taking one of Narnia's two pups . . . but how and who is going to take all of Portia's nine offspring?

The phone again. This time it's Joel. Excitement in his voice. "Do you know what, Dobbie? We can have Portia bred and sell her pedigreed pups for $200 a piece!"

Joel. Always the business man. "That's right," I tell him. "Maybe we can even pay for Melissa's braces."

"Let's see," his eight-year-old voice goes on, ignoring my irony, "a dog's first litter is usually small. So if she had nine this time, she should probably have twelve next time. Twelve times $200 is $2,400! Boy, oh boy!"

I can hear a dog, Sam, barking in the background.

So, wedged between storage cartons, I sit on the floor of the closet in the guest bedroom, files spilling forth their contents from the opened drawer, my search abandoned. Here I read my mother's words, hear my mother's voice, a voice lost to me. Her intonations, low and gentle, reach to me from beyond death. "Remember when?" she asks. "Remember when?" And the past comes rushing at me, sharply, taking my breath, growing larger, voluminous.

It comes back to me, the past in its wholeness. I look into my mother's face, hear once again her beautiful voice, and do so having, at long last, separated from her. I am my own self. There is a perimeter to my personality. It ends and no longer blends into that of the one who gave me life.

Seated in the closet, my thighs cradling the magic paper, I bow my forehead and touch it to my bent knees. I catch my breath. Something I had not understood, a tricky nuance, makes my heart lunge, my lungs draw a quick breath. During the time when my mother wrote her article, just a short while before her death, mother was individuating from me! She was making a life of her own, living less and less through me and my accomplishments. She was finding satisfactory fulfillment in, at last, seeing some of her own dreams come to fruition. One of her last efforts in life was to help me accomplish the painful transition she come-lately knew I would need to make.

And I know it now and I can hear the lilt in her laugh for the first time in ages, without the nagging need to create distance between us, to push her away.

Seated, my knees still cradling her creation, I bow my forehead and touch it once more to my knees, I feel the hard bones beneath the flesh. Longing fills my heart. And behind it all, behind it all, my mother's laughter. And I remember her. And I remember when.

PART V

A Community of Strangers

22

A Community of Strangers

I went to church one Sunday carrying a load of grief. Word had reached us that a Christian leader we admired, one we trusted, one whose integrity we had counted upon, had resigned his position after having committed adultery.

Adultery. The word wounded me. After months of following the national televangelist scandals, after months of hearing people poke fun at Christian things, after months of listening to disc jockeys use the media fiasco as an excuse to blaspheme our Lord, the fall of this respected minister was a blow to my soul. *Heartsick* is a good word to describe my state—heartsick. Word came one Saturday, after a committee meeting at church.

I went home, feeling as though a sudden, virulent case of influenza had overcome me. I told David the dreadful news then went to my bedroom and wept; wept for the man, his family—wept for all those who had loved and trusted his leadership. I wept for me. It is one thing when a celebrity figure fails in whom you have detected theological and psychological disorder; but it is another thing all together when a leader whom you respect fails. One's foundations shake. If this man can err, then perhaps one's own spiritual base might crumble.

Most of all, I wept for God. Some have said that God in His omnipotence doesn't need our tears. That may be so. Perhaps *I* need the tears. Perhaps I need to weep for God. Henri Nouwen in *The Genesee Diary* says: "Most remarkable is that this intimacy with God leads to a feeling that has never been part of my thinking but might be very important: Compassion for God." Nouwen quotes from the Jewish rabbi, Abraham Heschel, who tells of the Polish Jew who stopped praying "because of what happened in Auschwitz." Later, however, this Jew started to pray again. When asked, "What made you change your mind?" he answered, "It suddenly dawned upon me to think how lonely God must be; look with whom he is left. I felt very sorry for him."

Heschel continues: "Faith is the beginning of compassion, of compassion for God. It is when bursting with God's sighs that we are touched by the awareness that beyond all absurdity there is meaning, truth, and love."

So one Saturday I grieved for my friend the minister and for his wife; for his children coping with the shock of their father's confession of infidelity. But most of all I grieved for God. How we must disappoint Him—we to whom He has entrusted public leadership. What must God feel about the spiritual impoverishment of Christian leaders (my own spiritual impoverishment) in our needy days?

A sign of spiritual maturity is when we begin to use our own emotions and experiences to understand God's heart. Our own abandonment, for instance, helps us to know how God yearns after His loved ones who have turned away from Him. We learn "to Christify" our pain—*this is how Jesus must have felt after He was rejected by men*, we say to ourselves, after friends have failed us. Our suffering becomes redemptive in that we learn to understand God. This understanding intensifies our prayer, and we begin to live in a communion that is beyond the insular confines of our own private selves.

I had been a lonely woman; but looking back, I consider it a gift, a gift that helped me to consider others in this lonely world, a gift that made me sensitive toward God when all men despise Him, and when His spiritual children become prodigal.

Outwardly, I walked into our church the next Sunday morning composed and serene. I sat in my place in the pew and prayed for my husband. He was preaching that morning in another church; he was doing so despite being weary from overwork and dismayed by the dreadful news.

Then I began to notice those who surrounded me in the pews. Beside me sat a man who had undergone a recent spiritual renewal. On my other side sat a young woman home from the mission field of France; she had spent an evening at our dinner table that last week, and I had marveled at her faithful dedication in a hard place. At the far end of the pew sat a young man, a member of the small group I had been leading; beside them, my niece and her husband.

In front of me sat a woman who is part of the handful of us who meet regularly every Wednesday morning at seven o'clock for midweek worship and a healing service. Directly in front of me sat two darling boys and their father. This family had been guests in our home for a Lord's Day Eve celebration. I remembered their father's gentle blessing over each of them. Their mother is our church secretary, and she and I make a joyful ritual out of greeting each other with hugs and laughter at each new meeting.

The processional began and the congregation stood to sing the entrance hymn. "The Lord be with you," proclaimed the Celebrant. The corporate "you." *Together* we listened to the prayer for purity, *Almighty God, to you all hearts are open, all desires known, and from you no secrets are hid.* . . . Together we listened to the Old Testament reading, the Epistle, and the Gospel. As a congregation, we pronounced the Kyrie, "Lord have mercy, Christ have mercy. . . ." And I felt, despite my grief, how good it was at this troubled time to be among these people, in this familiar place.

Our rector stood to give the homily. This man had been a true pastor to me. He was one of the first in my adult life to offer me the gifts of Christ-like ministry. He allowed me enough latitude to work through pain and anger and misunderstanding in the privacy of his study. (I once provided a Kleenex box for his office to replace some of what I have used.) He has invited me, a woman, to serve on his church board and allowed me to express my odd and original gifts. He has tolerated my need to work out glitches in our relationship. And I have come to trust him.

His homily this morning reminded us that for the early disciples Christ was the reason for living and that without Christ, life simply didn't make sense. And my tears began to flow again as my heart struggled to affirm, *Yes, yes, it is Christ and no other.* It has never been human servants, neither man nor woman; never these feeble, finite, and frail creatures.

I sniffed. I hunted for a tissue. I tried not to be obvious, but all I could think was, *Oh God, how we have all disappointed you.* I blotted the tears so that my makeup wouldn't streak; I blew my nose. *Oh, God. Are there any of us whose lives give you pleasure?* I blinked, blew my nose again, wiped my eyes, struggling still to contain the emotion. *Oh, God, I grieve for you.*

The homily was over, and the congregation stood to repeat that ancient creedal affirmation. "We believe in one God," stated the congregation firmly, in one voice, united, "We believe. . . ." I have often wished we could rush the creed, abbreviate it; but now I understood something deeper about its meaning.

Here there was no faltering singular personal "I"; here there was no undone singular pronoun "me." No, here was the firm expression of the corporate pronoun *"we"* – that body of the very Christ about whom the homilist had been preaching. I could hear in my ear the strong, sure voices of the many, speaking as a whole, affirming the faith of the centuries, intoning as one the *we believe* of the ages. *"We*

believe in one Lord, Jesus Christ. . . . *We* believe in the Holy
Spirit, the Lord, the giver of life. . . . *We* believe. . . . *We* acknowledge. . . . *We* look for. . . ."

Alexander Schmemann, the Russian Orthodox priest,
writes that the meaning of the word *church* in Greek is "a
gathering" or "an assembly." He continues:

> When I say that I am going to church, it means that I am going
> into the assembly of the faithful in order, together with them,
> *to constitute the Church*. . . . The miracle of the church assembly
> lies in that it is not the "sum" of the sinful and unworthy
> people who comprise it, but the body of Christ.

No one leaned over and gave me a hug, no one patted my
hand or asked me if I would be all right; but I didn't need
them to. Their voices were in my ears. I was sustained by a
body standing together in corporate worship, a body of
people, many of whom I would never know, a body intoning
words of faith that insist on more belief than one person can
possibly affirm on her own for the long moments of a lifetime.
I was not alone. I was beginning to make significant connections with many of these people in these pews.

Christ came near to me that Sunday morning. His voice
reached me in the voices of many others, both friends and
strangers. His embrace touched me as the Peace of Christ
was shared in its passing—the time in the service when we
greet one another in the Lord's name. He sat beside me as
my neighbors, and I offered up the peoples' prayers. And I
affirmed again in my disappointed, wounded self—
surrounded by that body of people—that Christ is, has
always been and will always be the reason for my being.

The writer of Hebrews tells us in chapter 10, verses 23–25:
"Let us hold fast the confession of our hope without wavering, for he who promised is faithful; and let us consider how
to stir up one another to love and good works, not neglecting
to meet together, as is the habit of some, but encouraging

one another, and all the more as you see the Day drawing near" (RSV).

The people of St. Mark's parish have allowed me to become myself, to find my true self. I am not a public figure to them, a "celebrity." I am simply Karen Mains, small group member, housewife, mother, co-worker, wedding guest, committee co-chair, potluck planner, name on the church supper sign-up sheet, part of the cleaning crew, the last one on the prayer chain, Sunday school teacher. I am part of the life of this body.

I watch from my seat in the front pew, the drama at the communion rail. This one kneels who has given to me his most secret pain. This young woman who lifts her crossed palms is making a long journey into faith. This man is lonely; as he takes the chalice to his lips, I realize we have shared a common cup. My struggles and successes are known to them; their pain and joys are known to me. We share a common life. They have let me into this circle of love. I do not want to excommunicate myself from them in any way. I am joined to them by this life in Christ we share.

So let us enter the sanctuary, sit beside other believers, brothers and sisters in Christ, the people we know, those in this life we will never know. Let us open our Bible. Let us sing the hymns and confess, "we believe." Let us be aware that the we believe of the church of God is being pronounced in hundreds of churches throughout this land and worldwide—in thousands of little thatched-roofed, bamboo-sided, clay-daubed buildings; in great cathedrals; in city store-fronts; in prisons; in secret shelters; on hillsides; beneath banyan trees. Every Sabbath, the we believe begins in the voices of God's people and traverses every time zone, out from the prime meridian at Greenwich in England and back again. "We believe . . . we believe . . . we believe. . . ."

Let us think about the church through the centuries, to those who have died for the sake of the *we believe*. Let us think ahead to the generations yet unborn, to those who too will stand some place and say with all their hearts, "We believe. . . ." Let us listen to the anthem of this chorus. Let us imagine the song joined by the company of heaven; let us think of the holy ones, the angelic beings who shout as well, *"We believe."*

Let us go to church, disappointed perhaps, grieving perhaps, lonely and afraid. Then, let us forget ourselves and remember that we are part of a great company of friends and strangers, a company broader, vaster than we can fathom, a company which sustains us even when we neglect it or are unaware of its sustaining action in our lives. Let us understand that where we are weak, others strengths will make us strong; where others are weak, our courage will strengthen them.

Then let us find compassion in our hearts for this great God who endures our infidelities, our foibles, our imperfections and failings. Let us remind one another that He loves this great company—"the ones with whom He is left." Then let us speak again, realizing we are part of this broader whole, this awkward, precious company of faith. Let us say the words with our dying breaths: *We believe.*